THE PILGRIMS' WAY

THE PILGRIMS' WAY

TO CANTERBURY FROM WINCHESTER AND LONDON

by Leigh Hatts

JUNIPER HOUSE, MURLEY MOSS,
OXENHOLME ROAD, KENDAL, CUMBRIA LA9 7RL
www.cicerone.co.uk

© Leigh Hatts 2017
First edition 2017
Reprinted 2018, 2021, 2024 (with updates)
ISBN-13: 978 1 85284 777 7

Printed in Czechia on behalf of Latitude Press Ltd on responsibly sourced paper
A catalogue record for this book is available from the British Library.

© Crown copyright and database rights 2017 OS AC0000810376
All photographs are by the author unless otherwise stated.

Acknowledgements

The author is grateful for advice on the Canterbury routes from his wife Marion Marples, former secretary of the Confraternity of Saint James which promotes the Camino de Santiago, who accompanied him on the Pilgrims' Way.

Updates to this Guide

While every effort is made by our authors to ensure the accuracy of guidebooks as they go to print, changes can occur during the lifetime of an edition. Any updates that we know of for this guide will be on the Cicerone website (www.cicerone.co.uk/777/updates), so please check before planning your trip. We also advise that you check information about such things as transport, accommodation and shops locally. Even rights of way can be altered over time. We are always grateful for information about any discrepancies between a guidebook and the facts on the ground, sent by email to updates@cicerone.co.uk.

Register your book: To sign up to receive free updates, special offers and GPX files where available, create a Cicerone account and register your purchase via the 'My Account' tab at www.cicerone.co.uk.

Front cover: Geoffrey Chaucer window by CE Kempe in Southwark Cathedral

CONTENTS

Map key 6
Route summary table 7

INTRODUCTION 11
History of the Way 12
Renewed interest 14
Historical figures along the Way 16
Variations to the Way 19
Walking the Way 21
When to walk 22
Where to stay 23
Refreshments 24
Waymarking 24
Maps 25
Using this guide 25

WINCHESTER TO CANTERBURY 27
Stage 1   Winchester to Alresford 28
Stage 2   Alresford to Alton 38
Stage 3   Alton to Farnham 47
Stage 4   Farnham to Guildford 57
Stage 5   Guildford to Box Hill 66
Stage 6   Box Hill to Merstham 78
Stage 7   Merstham to Oxted 87
Stage 8   Oxted to Otford 95
Stage 9   Otford to Wrotham 103
Stage 10   Wrotham to Halling 108
Stage 11   Halling to Aylesford 115
Stage 11a   Peters Village to Rochester 122
Stage 12   Aylesford to Harrietsham 129
Stage 13   Harrietsham to Boughton Lees 139
Stage 14   Boughton Lees to Chilham 149
Stage 15   Chilham to Canterbury 156

LONDON ROUTE 165
Stage 1a   Southwark to Shooters Hill 166
Stage 2a   Shooters Hill to Dartford 175
Stage 3a   Dartford to Otford 185

Appendix A   Itinerary planner 196
Appendix B   Accommodation 199
Appendix C   Further information 202
Appendix D   Further reading 203

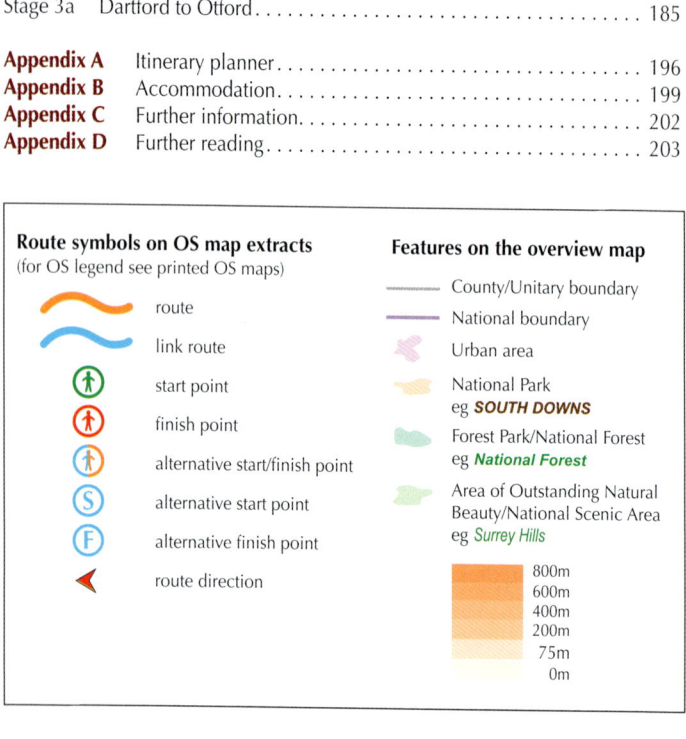

ROUTE SUMMARY TABLE

Stage	Distance	Time	Page
1 Winchester to Alresford	9 miles (14.4km)	5hrs	28
2 Alresford to Alton	12 miles (19.3km)	5hrs	38
3 Alton to Farnham	11 miles (17.7km)	5hrs	47
4 Farnham to Guildford	10½ miles (16.8km)	4hrs	57
5 Guildford to Box Hill	13½ miles (21.7km)	6hrs	66
6 Box Hill to Merstham	9¾ miles (15.6km)	3½hrs	78
7 Merstham to Oxted	8 miles (12.8km)	3hrs	87
8 Oxted to Otford	12 miles (19.3km)	5hrs	95
9 Otford to Wrotham	5¾ miles (9.2km)	2½hrs	103
10 Wrotham to Halling	7¼ miles (11.6km)	3½hrs	108
11 Halling to Aylesford	4¾ miles (7.6km)	2hrs	115
11a Peters Village to Rochester	4½ miles (7.2km)	1¾hrs	122
12 Aylesford to Harrietsham	11 miles (17.7km)	4½hrs	129
13 Harrietsham to Boughton Lees	11 miles (17.7km)	4½hrs	139
14 Boughton Lees to Chilham	6 miles (9.6km)	2¼hrs	149
15 Chilham to Canterbury	7 miles (11.2km)	2½hrs	156
London Route			
1a Southwark to Shooters Hill	8½ miles (13.6km)	4hrs	166
2a Shooters Hill to Dartford	13 miles (21km)	5½hrs	175
3a Dartford to Otford	11½ miles (18.5km)	5hrs	185

Southwark Cathedral above Borough Market

THE PILGRIMS' WAY

Thomas Becket window at Dartford Church

INTRODUCTION

The Pilgrims' Way (PW) to Canterbury Cathedral begins in Winchester, with an alternative starting point at Southwark in London. These ancient paths, which eventually merge, became famous around AD1200 when pilgrims first started making the journey (on horseback and on foot) to the tomb of martyred St Thomas Becket in Canterbury.

The route from Winchester follows part of a major landscape feature of southern England, a chalk ridge extending from the Ridgeway in the west to the white cliffs of Dover in the east. From Farnham to Canterbury the ridge is part of the North Downs, which act as a barrier on the approach to London and to the Thames valley from the south coast.

The main towns along the way are found where the ridge is broken by rivers such as the Itchen at Winchester, the Wey at Guildford and the Mole at Dorking. The Pilgrims' Way for the most part follows a terrace on the south side of the ridge, along the spring line, where the villages, churches and pubs are found.

The Pilgrims' Way passing the scenic River Itchen (Stage 1)

THE PILGRIMS' WAY

HISTORY OF THE WAY

The pilgrimage stems from the fatal stabbing of Archbishop of Canterbury Thomas Becket in 1170. Becket was Lord Chancellor and a close confidant of King Henry II who decided that his relations with the Church would improve if his trusted friend Thomas filled the vacancy for archbishop. The reluctant Becket was prevailed on to be ordained priest and consecrated bishop at unprecedented speed. However, once installed, Becket decided that his loyalty lay with the Church rather than the King. Eventually, in anger, Henry called out 'Who shall rid me of this troublesome priest?' Six knights mistakenly took this outburst as an order and set out for Canterbury.

The murder of Archbishop Becket took place at dusk in the north transept of Canterbury Cathedral on Tuesday 29 December. The joyful Christmas octave Vespers had already begun. Suddenly, appalling bloodshed shook the Canterbury monastic community, which was changed forever. The news reached London the next day and the King of France learnt about it on the Friday. The Pope, who was living at Anagni, south of Rome, was told in early February.

For an era of slow communication the reaction was fast. Becket was canonised after just three years. In 1174 Henry II went to Canterbury as a barefoot pilgrim, and in Spain a chapel in Toledo Cathedral was dedicated to the saint. The next year Salamanca built

A candle marks the site of Thomas Becket's shrine (Stage 15)

the first church dedicated to Thomas. Other Becket chapels followed within the decade, including one in 1180 at Lyon in France. By 1191 the devotion had spread to Hungary with a St Thomas church in Esztergom. Yet another opened in Catania in Sicily in 1179.

In England St Thomas chapels were attached to monasteries at Peterborough and Waltham Abbey. London Bridge was rebuilt with the Chapel of St-Thomas-on-the-Bridge added to the middle downstream side, while Southwark Priory, at the bridge's south end, rededicated its public infirmary as the Hospital of St Thomas of Canterbury. Today St Thomas' Hospital is upstream, opposite the Houses of Parliament.

Europe's largest foundation in Becket's honour was Arbroath Abbey, which William I of Scotland, who had known the English archbishop, had dedicated in 1178. There was substantial pilgrimage south to Canterbury, sometimes via Rochester, where Scottish St William of Perth was buried. Indeed, Perth also had a devotion to Becket.

It appears that pilgrimage to Canterbury from London and Winchester began as early as 1172 and grew rapidly to be maintained over almost 500 years. Pilgrims included Louis VII of France just nine years after the murder, Alexander II of Scotland in 1223 and his widowed queen in 1276. By this time Edward I was a regular pilgrim and Holy Roman Emperor Charles V went in 1520. However, within 18 years Henry VIII had destroyed the shrine during the Reformation upheaval and banned all liturgical commemoration of Becket, as he was an archbishop who had defied a king.

The Pilgrims' Way from Winchester to Canterbury became a track which was mainly recognised only locally until the 19th century. By the 1790s Surrey antiquary William Bray had identified two stretches. In 1855 *The Pilgrims Way or Path towards the Shrine of St Thomas of Canterbury* by Albert Way was published with the support of the Dean of Canterbury.

Towards the end of the century the routes were being explored by others. In 1885 Americans Elizabeth and Joseph Pennell published *A Canterbury Pilgrimage* which described their ride on a tandem tricycle from London to Canterbury. A decade later Julia Cartwright's book *The Pilgrims' Way from Winchester to Canterbury* ran into several editions. Hilaire Belloc, who published *The Old Road* in 1904, walked from Winchester during Christmas week 1899 starting on 22 December and arriving in Canterbury on St Thomas Becket's Day, 29 December. He believed that yew trees often found lining the route were significant markers. Cartwright and Belloc were intrigued by Ordnance Survey® maps which marked a route in gothic type. However, this was largely conjecture on the part of OS surveyor Edward Renouard James, who in 1871 wrote about the Pilgrims' Way in Surrey and was encouraged by OS director and enthusiastic historian Sir Henry James. There is not a definitive continuous route since the various map editions disagree in several places in identifying the old way.

Pilgrims may have already been using the route in Becket's lifetime to visit St Augustine's Abbey at Canterbury, where a well-promoted shrine commemorated St Augustine, who brought Christianity to Kent in 597. However, the road is probably older than Augustine's arrival as it is believed that it had been used by the Romans. Along with the Icknield Way this is one of the first real national trails.

RENEWED INTEREST

Interest in Becket had never died. In 1935 TS Eliot's *Murder in the Cathedral* was premiered in the chapter house of Canterbury Cathedral thanks to the support of Dean Hewlett Johnson. A screen version by Austrian film director George Hoellering was released in 1951. Actors included Leo McKern, with Becket played by well-known priest John Groser. Earlier, the 1944 film *A Canterbury Tale* mixed a World War II story on the ancient route with tales of pilgrims. In 1964 Richard Burton took the lead role in the film *Becket*. These productions heightened interest in Thomas Becket.

However, most influential was Nevill Coghill's modern English translation of Geoffrey Chaucer's work which became the basis for the award-winning *Canterbury Tales* musical written with Martin Starkie. It played to packed houses in the West End and on Broadway during the late 1960s.

The 1947 Hobhouse Report on footpaths and countryside access recommended reviving the Pilgrims' Way as a walkers' recreational route. As a result the North Downs Way (NDW) was devised and in 1978 the Archbishop of Canterbury Donald Coggan was invited to perform the official opening. But the NDW only utilises parts of the Pilgrims' Way and begins in Surrey. Indeed, the launch ceremony took place on the Wye Downs where the national trail heads for Dover rather than Canterbury.

In the 21st century Canterbury Cathedral has pilgrim pages on its website in response to an increasing number of foot pilgrims. Seventy years after the Hobhouse Report this guidebook has been written to help intending pilgrims who seek to experience the authentic Pilgrims' Way starting from either Winchester or London.

St Thomas of Canterbury was officially restored to the Church of England calendar in 1980. 'St Thomas is now very much a shared saint across the denominations, a figure of unity rather than division allowing us to go beyond that turmoil of the 16th century which resulted in the destruction

LITERARY CONNECTIONS TO THE WAY

Geoffrey Chaucer
Geoffrey Chaucer's fictional work *The Canterbury Tales*, written at the end of the 14th century, features 24 stories told by imaginary pilgrim characters on their way from Southwark at the south end of London Bridge to Canterbury. One is the Wife of Bath who has already been on pilgrimage to Santiago de Compostela. Chaucer's book was the first to be printed by William Caxton when he set up his press in 1476 and it proved so popular that another edition followed in 1483.

TS Eliot
Written in 1935 for Canterbury Cathedral, Eliot's *Murder in the Cathedral* is a play telling the story of Thomas Becket, and dramatic extracts are still recited at Canterbury on the anniversary of Becket's murder. In 1953 it was staged at The Old Vic theatre in London and more recently in Southwark Cathedral.

Jane Austen
The novelist knew many places along the Pilgrims' Way although she never mentions it. She is buried in Winchester Cathedral's north aisle where there is a stained glass window commemorating her. She died in the city in 1817, having lived in Chawton from 1809 where she wrote many of her novels. Chevening, where her cousin was rector, is probaby the original Rosings Park in *Pride and Prejudice*. Jane had stayed nearby before her cousin was appointed. *Emma* features a picnic on Box Hill and its character Miss Bates is based on a lady who lived in Cathedral House within Canterbury Cathedral precincts.

Jane Austen's house (Stage 2)

Jane stayed with her brother Edward at Godmersham from where she visited Chilham for a ball and went shopping in Canterbury. On travelling to Kent she stayed at the Bull & George in Dartford and in Lenham and Wrotham where clergy relatives were incumbents. Her brother Henry was curate at Chawton and, after her death in 1817, also at Farnham and Bentley.

of the shrine,' claims priest and historian Nicholas Schofield, who followed the route from London for the 2015 film *To Be A Pilgrim: The Canterbury Way*. 'There have been many positive developments in recent years and the pilgrimage to Canterbury is itself enjoying something of a revival.'

HISTORICAL FIGURES ALONG THE WAY

In addition to St Thomas of Canterbury the following significant figures feature more than once in churches, towns and villages:

St Swithun

St Swithun is Winchester's own saint. He was born in the city and became its bishop in 852. After his death 10 years later he was buried outside the minster, the outline of which can be found to the north of the cathedral. When on 15 July 971 his remains were moved inside the minster there was a violent storm and days of rain followed. This gave rise to the legend that the weather on his feast day, 15 July, rain or sunshine, would be the norm until St Bartholomew's Day on 24 August 40 days later. August is often mainly dry or rainy and weather patterns indicate occasional truth in the saying when the 40 days is applied to the old calendar which places St Swithun's Day on what is now 26 July and St Bartholomew's Day on 4 September. He is patron saint of droughts.

St Swithun's Shrine showing the side of the canopy depicting rain

HISTORICAL FIGURES ALONG THE WAY

In 1006 Bishop of Winchester St Alphege, who had been made archbishop, took Swithun's head with him to Canterbury and it is now in Evreux Cathedral in Normandy. In about 1128 a monk took one of Swithun's arms to Norway where Stavanger Cathedral is dedicated to St Swithun. The remaining bones were lost in 1538 when Thomas Cromwell destroyed the shrine in Winchester Cathedral on Henry VIII's orders. Today a canopy depicting sun and rain marks its location. Swithun is often depicted in churches holding a model bridge because he built the first over the River Itchen.

St James the Great

This is a popular church dedication and his image with pilgrim scallop shell symbol, staff and water bottle appears in many church windows. He is one of the 12 Apostles and also the pilgrim saint since his decapitated body lies in Santiago de Compostela in north-west Spain, which is the climax of a great pilgrimage route attracting thousands on foot every year.

Gundulf

The Norman Benedictine monk from Bec was Bishop of Rochester from 1077 to 1108. He is best known for his association with building projects including the Tower of London for William the Conqueror. In the Rochester Diocese he rebuilt the cathedral and Dartford church, and at Trottiscliffe church he added a house for himself. Halling Palace on the River Medway was intended for overnight stops on the way to Canterbury. He acted as the Archbishop's deputy and was in charge during a four-year vacancy at Canterbury. Property secured by Gundulf included the manor of Lambeth where Lambeth Palace, the archbishop's London home, was built a century later.

Henry de Blois

Bishop Henry de Blois, William the Conqueror's grandson and King Stephen's brother, was a Cluny monk who served simultaneously as Abbot of Glastonbury and Bishop of Winchester (1129–71). For a time (1139–43) he was also papal legate, which meant that he took precedence over the Archbishop of Canterbury. He built the palace at Southwark along with Farnham Castle to be the halfway house on the route from Winchester. After visiting Rome he went on pilgrimage to Santiago de Compostela. An early supporter of Becket, de Blois presided over his election and consecration as archbishop in 1162. Bishop de Blois's house next to Southwark Cathedral was made available to Becket on his last visit just weeks before his death. The Bishop of Winchester died the following year having rebuked the King for his behaviour towards Becket. His simple but prominent tomb is between the choir stalls in Winchester Cathedral.

Cardinal Henry Beaufort

John of Gaunt's son was Bishop of Winchester from 1404 until his death in 1447. One of his periods as Lord Chancellor coincided with the Battle of Agincourt for which he personally loaned £2000. His magnificent tomb in Winchester Cathedral is next to St Swithun's shrine which, thanks to Beaufort's wealth, was moved a few yards to its present site in 1476. He made a pilgrimage to Santiago de Compostela and presided at the trial of Joan of Arc who gave him her ring before she was burnt. His figure can be found on the high altar screens in both Winchester and Southwark cathedrals. A colourful carving of his heraldic shield with cardinal's hat is in Southwark's south transept. He also built the Old Vicarage in Farnham churchyard, once used as a pilgrim hostel.

Bishop Richard Fox

The founder of Corpus Christi College, Oxford, Fox was Bishop of Winchester from 1501 until his death in 1528. As Lord Privy Seal he was heavily involved in national affairs. He baptised the future Henry VIII and negotiated the marriage of Katharine of Aragon to Henry's older brother Prince Arthur. His brick building work at Farnham Castle survives, as do the steps down into town built for him in old age. His magnificent chantry tomb decorated with his pelican crest is close to St Swithun's shrine in Winchester Cathedral.

St Thomas More

Lord Chancellor until he declined to support Henry VIII's desire for a divorce from Katharine of Aragon, More claimed to be 'the king's good servant but God's first'. This echoed the reply of Becket, also Lord Chancellor, to Henry II: 'We ought to obey God rather than man.' More was executed in 1535 at the Tower of London and his body buried in the chapel while his head was displayed on the Southwark gateway to London Bridge. His daughter Margaret Roper arranged for the gatekeeper to throw the head down to a boat where she waited with her skirt held out. The head is now in a vault at St Dunstan's church in Canterbury near to the Roper residence, which are both on the Pilgrims' Way. The family later lived at Farningham on the pilgrim road from London. Thomas More died a year before Henry VIII suppressed the observance of the St Thomas Becket feast day.

St John Fisher

The Bishop of Rochester, St John Fisher, often stayed at his Halling house by the River Medway. His support for Katharine of Aragon brought him into conflict with Henry VIII. On 21 May 1535 the bishop was made a cardinal. On hearing that Fisher had been given a red hat, the king vowed that he would never have a head to put it on and had him executed on 22 June just a fortnight before Thomas More. For a time both heads were

Thomas More window at St Dunstan's church in Canterbury

displayed on London Bridge. The feast of St John Fisher and St Thomas More is observed on 22 June.

Thomas Cubitt

The early 19th-century master builder lived at Denbies on the Pilgrims' Way near Box Hill and masterminded the great housing estates of Belgravia and Pimlico in London and Kemp Town in Brighton. He opened his own brickworks on the Pilgrims' Way near Aylesford.

St Oscar Romero

The Archbishop of San Salvador from 1977 was assassinated in 1980 while celebrating Mass. The previous day he had criticised the government. In St George's Roman Catholic Cathedral in Southwark (opposite the Imperial War Museum) there is a memorial to this 20th-century archbishop martyr in the form of a huge three-dimensional painted Salvadoran Cross. Appropriately, the cathedral also has a small Becket relic. The Church of St Thomas of Canterbury at Canterbury shows Romero's vestments alongside Becket relics. Like Thomas More, Romero is a Becket-like martyr.

VARIATIONS TO THE WAY

The Winchester–Canterbury route is the original Pilgrims' Way. This was used by travellers from the west of England and visitors from the continent who had arrived at Southampton or Portsmouth (which from 1188 had a St Thomas chapel, now a cathedral). Hilaire Belloc suggests that pilgrims came to Canterbury from Devon and Cornwall, Brittany, Spain and Portugal via Winchester. But of course people in London did not wish to go via Winchester, nor did visitors to England who had sailed up the River Thames. They left the capital by way of the Roman Watling Street and joined the other route either south of Dartford or after Rochester. Chaucer's route is from London by way of Rochester joining the Winchester route just outside Canterbury.

Link to Rochester

This guide includes a riverside link to Rochester from the Medway crossing point (see Stage 11a). Rochester can, of course, be a third starting point for those wanting a shorter walk but it is still a traditional route.

In medieval times most pilgrims from London would have continued to Canterbury along the most direct route, Roman Watling Street. At Faversham they could stay at the now lost abbey, or nearby at Ospringe where the 13th-century Maison Dieu can still be visited. But this route is now a not so pleasant major traffic corridor.

Walking from Winchester

For the first few miles there is little evidence of the old road, so the route now used as far as Farnham is based on the 2002 St Swithun's Way. Beyond Hampshire this guide resists the temptation to revert to the 20th-century NDW. Sometimes the national trail handily coincides with the ancient way. Wherever the Pilgrims' Way has not become a busy main road and remains publicly accessible it is the route to be taken.

Walking from London

The route from London was first a Roman road much used not just by those passing between the capital and Canterbury but also by visitors to London from abroad who arrived at Dover. The starting point in the capital was always Southwark at the south end of London Bridge. The crossing, with houses and shops, was closed at night so it was considered best to seek a bed in one of the numerous Southwark inns to be ready to make an early unimpeded getaway at first light.

This guide retains as much as possible of the first few miles of the ancient Roman road from Southwark. Where the present pilgrim route leaves the old main road it goes, as a pilgrim might have, via Lesnes Abbey which is dedicated to the saint. After Dartford many travellers and pilgrims turned south to join the Winchester–Canterbury Pilgrims' Way at Otford and so this guide takes the walker up the Darenth Valley where the archbishop held land and first fell out with the king.

Southwark is part of Winchester

Southwark, in London, can be described as being part of Winchester.

WALKING THE WAY

Southwark Cathedral window: Chaucer pilgrims leaving the Tabard inn

It was within the vast Winchester Diocese which lay south of the River Thames and the bishop had his London home next to Southwark Priory (now Cathedral). The remains of the Winchester Palace dining hall can still be seen in Clink Street. The palace parkland ran west to embrace the site of the Tate Modern gallery. The priory church began as a convent founded by Winchester; Bishop Richard Fox gave it an east end stone screen similar to the one found at Winchester. Other Winchester bishops, such as Cardinal Beaufort and Lancelot Andrewes, are commemorated or buried in the church. The nearby Tabard inn, from where pilgrims including Chaucer's characters set out, was owned by Winchester's Hyde Abbey and used as a lodging by the abbot when visiting the capital. Queen Mary married Philip of Spain in Winchester Cathedral and afterwards came to Southwark to dine at the bishop's house before entering the City of London. Today Winchester Wharf is on the riverside, and inland there are Winchester Cottages, Winchester Arms flats and Winchester House.

WALKING THE WAY

Backpacking the PW

The best experience must be to walk from Winchester or London in one

THE PILGRIMS' WAY

go. The long route from Winchester to Canterbury is 138 miles and might take two weeks. The 85-mile way from London Bridge would require about a week, while pilgrims starting at Rochester could reach Canterbury over three days by covering the 34 miles while still having time to pause at viewpoints and churches.

Day trips

Some people will find it more convenient to undertake day trips or weekend breaks to slowly achieve the full distance. This is similar to how many busy people walk to Santiago de Compostela completing stretches a fortnight at a time over several years.

Setting out and arriving

The pilgrim passport is called a pilgrim record and is available from the Winchester, Southwark and Rochester cathedral shops. It can be stamped at churches, pubs, hostels and hotels on the route. Some places will have their own local Pilgrims' Way stamp.

Admission to Southwark and Rochester cathedrals is free. At Winchester any pilgrims wishing to start at St Swithun's shrine are asked to give advance notice to obtain free admission (See Stage 1).

At Canterbury Cathedral free admission is normally available on presentation of a stamped pilgrim record.

WHEN TO WALK

It is natural to want to undertake a long walk in summer when it is warm and the daylight lasts into evening. Chaucer suggests April. However, there is much evidence that pilgrims also walked in winter, especially during Christmas to arrive at Canterbury on St Thomas Becket's Day, 29 December. There are some who walk at this same time across northern Spain in December to be in Santiago Cathedral on 30 December for the Translation of St James the Great. At this time accommodation is not always easily available. The way is walkable in winter although it may be muddy or flooded in places after heavy rain.

Canterbury special days

There are several special days in Canterbury marking significant dates relating to Becket. The murder in 1170 is recalled vividly at the cathedral on its anniversary on 29 December with early morning and late evening services. During evensong there is a liturgical re-enactment of Becket's final moments using readings from TS Eliot's *Murder in the Cathedral*. The gathering is in the Quire, usually with the Archbishop presiding, before the congregation, with candles, moves to the Martyrdom site. Here, at the Altar of the Sword's Point, incense is used during the singing of the Magnificat. As an excerpt from the play is read, the cloister doors are banged shut and then, at Becket's cry 'throw open the doors!', thrown open. The body was taken to the crypt afterwards so later the day of commemoration ends with Vespers sung in the Undercroft.

In summer the special days are 6, 7 and 12 July. The first is the anniversary of St Thomas More's execution which is marked in the evening by a service, with an address by a historian, at St Dunstan's church. The following day, 7 July, is the Translation of St Thomas Becket with special services recalling the moving of the saint's body in 1220 from the crypt up to a new shrine. At evensong the Dean and Chapter, the monks' successors, and pilgrims gather round the shrine site. The third day, 12 July, is the anniversary of Henry II's penitential pilgrimage in 1174 when he walked barefoot from St Dunstan's to the cathedral.

WHERE TO STAY

Accommodation is at present uneven along the Pilgrims' Way. Towns and south-east London offer a choice, but with pub closures not every village, especially in Surrey, has handy bed and breakfast facilities. It is advisable to book ahead. Bed and breakfast accommodation is briefly mentioned at the start of each stage. For more details of accommodation see Appendix B. The British Pilgrimage Trust website (britishpilgrimage.org) includes an interactive Pilgrims' Way map indicating accommodation (see Appendix C).

Lavender field near Shoreham

THE PILGRIMS' WAY

Clockwise from top: Old PW sign at Chaldon; St Swithun's Way logo at Alton; PW sign near Charing; Street sign & PO box at Marley

REFRESHMENTS

On certain stages where there are few pubs, or you prefer not to turn into a village, it would be wise to take food. It is always sensible to take water whatever the season. Some pubs, mainly in Kent, serve Bishops Finger ale named after the Pilgrims' Way finger posts.

WAYMARKING

Dedicated Pilgrims' Way markers are rare. Where it coincides with the modern St Swithun's Way and North Downs Way then waymarking is good. The pilgrim symbol is a scallop shell although this is mostly associated with the Camino of St James in Spain. From Winchester to Farnham the familiar waymark is the St Swithun's Way shell with two croziers representing St Swithun and St Thomas Becket. Churches along the route often have a stone with a shell motif in the churchyard wall as part of a millennium project. Pilgrims' Way signposts marked with a shell were erected in Kent as

USING THIS GUIDE

part of the 1951 Festival of Britain but were not maintained. A large carved wooden scallop can be found on the ancient gatehouse doorway where pilgrims are welcomed at Canterbury Cathedral.

MAPS

The OS maps covering the Pilgrims' Way are:
OS Explorer® series: OL32, OL33, 144, 145, 146, 147, 148, 137, 150, 173, 161, 162
Landranger® series: 185, 186, 187, 188, 178, 189, 179, 177

The map(s) needed for each specific stage are detailed in the information box at the start of the stage description.

USING THIS GUIDE

An information box at the beginning of each stage gives the start and finish points, approximate walking time and distance along the Pilgrims' Way (not including links to railway stations), transport links (with distance to and from the route), details of OS Explorer maps, food and, where possible, accommodation. Look at the

Guildford High Street and St Nicholas church (Stage 5)

next stage for accommodation when ending a walk.

Each stage also has a short introduction offering a feel of the route and highlighting any landmarks. Features that appear on the extract from the 1:50,000 OS maps that accompany the route descriptions are highlighted in bold, to help you to follow your progress on the map.

The distances for each stage should be achievable in one day, although the day can often be curtailed at a village with accommodation or served by bus or railway. The fall back is a taxi to a transport hub or accommodation.

Estimated times for stages are generous to allow for enjoying the view, visiting churches and resting in pubs, which are an important part of the experience.

The maps for Stages 1a and 2a are at the scale 1:50,000 but are zoomed in to a scale of 1:25,000 (it is still 1km between the blue grid lines of course). The map for Stage 1a, the first stage out of London, is highlighted with numbers to help the reader locate landmarks along the road in the dense busy city centre.

An itinerary planner has been provided (see Appendix A) listing train stations, refreshments and accommodation options for each stage, as has a route summary table, detailing the distance and estimated duration of each stage.

Winchester to Canterbury is 138 miles (222km). Southwark, at London Bridge, to Canterbury is 75 miles (120km).

Stile at Old Down Wood (Stage 2)

STAGE 1
Winchester to Alresford

Start	Winchester Cathedral
Finish	The Cricketers, Alresford
Distance	9 miles (14.4km)
Time	5hrs
Maps	OS Explorer OL32; Landranger 185
Refreshments	Winchester Cathedral Refectory; pubs at Kings Worthy, Itchen Abbas and Ovington
Public transport	Railway station at Winchester; bus at Alresford
Accommodation	Winchester

The PW begins in a busy city with a feel and size which will not be found again until Canterbury. The first landmark is Hyde Abbey on the edge of the old city. But beyond there is almost immediate countryside and after Kings Worthy, the first village with a church and pub, there is a rural remoteness until Alresford is reached. This country town, like Winchester, owes much to early Bishops of Winchester.

From Winchester station
Go down the hill and ahead along City Road, right into Jewry Street, left into the traffic-free High Street and right under the arch at the Butter Cross to see the cathedral (½ mile/0.8km).

WINCHESTER

Hampshire's county town was a Roman city. King Alfred, who rebuilt the city as the Wessex capital, opened a mint here and the origins of the Treasury can be traced to here. Near the west gate is the Great Hall, the only surviving part of the Norman castle, where a circular table top known as King Arthur's round table is displayed on a wall. The Butter Cross, or city cross, in the High Street dates from 1427 and the shops behind were the 'Hevene' and 'Helle'

Stage 1 – Winchester to Alresford

taverns, familiar to pilgrims passing between the two. A curfew bell is rung from Lloyds Bank, the old Guildhall, at 8pm.

Successor to a Saxon building, Winchester Cathedral was begun in 1079 and early pilgrims came to venerate St Birinus. By 1200 there were so many pilgrims to St Swithun's shrine that the east end was extended. West of the shrine site is a tiny door, known as the Holy Hole, which led to the location of Swithun's relics before a final short move in 1476. The crypt, dug deep into the water meadows, is prone to flooding and has a statue of a diver by Anthony Gormley which is often surrounded by water. The cathedral's Benedictine community was dissolved in 1539. Fifteen years later Queen Mary chose to be married here to Philip of Spain on St James's Day, 25 July. Outside in the close is the Pilgrims' Hall, with an early hammerbeam roof, dating from about 1300. Beyond the gateway opposite is a second gateway where tiny St Swithun's Church is situated above the roadway.

Pilgrims wishing to start at St Swithun's shrine in the cathedral should contact the reception (preferably by phoning in advance 01962 857200) to ensure free entry and a formal sending off by the canon-in-residence or another staff member. Pilgrim records are obtainable from the cathedral shop next to the refectory.

From the cathedral's west door bear half right past the Rifle Corps memorial (right) and down the avenue of trees to enter the narrow street known as The Square. Pass tiny St Lawrence Church (right) and go through an arch to the High Street. Go right past the Butter Cross and then left at WH Smith, which has a rustic frontage.

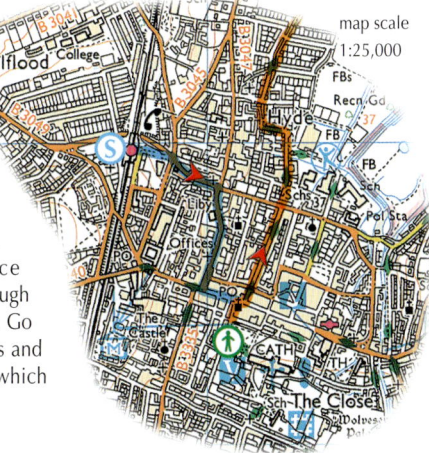

map scale 1:25,000

The Pilgrims' Way

Cross over St George's Street (pelican crossing) and continue down Parchment Street to North Walls Road. Use the pelican crossing to the right to enter the car park opposite. Walk to the far end and turn left to meet Gordon Road at a bend. Go right to pass St Bede's School (right) and St Valentines Close (left) and cross a stream (a branch of the River Itchen), on the boundary of the lost Hyde Abbey.

Hyde Abbey was built in about 1110 for monks forced out of the New Minster (cathedral) by continual disputes over singing and insanitary conditions. Hyde's own pilgrim attraction was the head of St Valentine which had been given by Canute's Queen Emma, mother of Edward the Confessor. The abbey was dissolved in 1538 but an inner gateway survives opposite St Bartholomew's, built for the abbey's lay people. This was extended and a tower added using stone from the monastery. The churchyard is thought to hold the body of King Alfred. The sanctuary of the demolished abbey church is seen in outline at the east end of King Alfred Place which runs down the nave. The abbey owned the Tabard inn in Southwark (see London Stage 1a) where Chaucer set the opening of *The Canterbury Tales*.

At the end of Gordon Road go left up King Alfred Terrace to cross the water again. Bear right along a path to reach King Alfred Place. The abbey gatehouse and St Bartholomew's are to the left. The road to the right, beyond the stream, leads to the abbey church site.

The King Alfred pub stands on the northern boundary of the abbey grounds.

The PW continues ahead down Saxon Road. ◄ Before the sharp bend ahead go right into Nuns Road to cross the stream. At once go left to keep the water to the left.

Beyond a road, the way, known here as Nuns Walk, becomes rough and soon joins a wider track. At **Abbotts Barton**, where there are willows, the path changes bank. There are soon views across water meadows. After crossing a bridge, the path comes up against a main road. Bear left on a straight path to find a tunnel running under two

STAGE 1 – WINCHESTER TO ALRESFORD

roads. The path turns left to a gate. Follow the way through a small industrial estate and pass bow-fronted houses overlooking the green at **Kings Worthy**. Keep forward to enter the churchyard where the path leads to the church's west door.

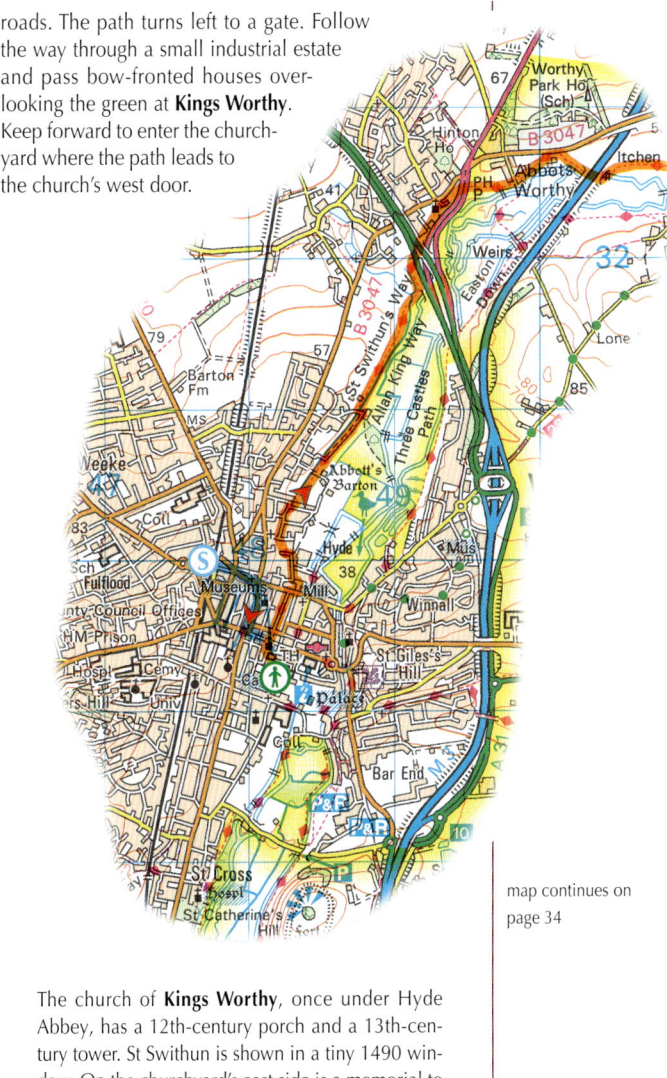

map continues on page 34

The church of **Kings Worthy**, once under Hyde Abbey, has a 12th-century porch and a 13th-century tower. St Swithun is shown in a tiny 1490 window. On the churchyard's east side is a memorial to

Open Spaces Society founder Lord Eversley who as postmaster general started the parcel post.

Walk along the north side of the church and past Chestnut Cottage to bear half right into St Mary's Close between the Old Post Office (left) and Tavern Cottage (right). ◄ Pass between two garages and under an apple tree by Eversley Cottage (left) to reach Albert's Gate. Cross the usually busy dual carriageway. Ahead, a footpath leads down into woods, crossing a sometimes dry stream to reach Abbotsworthy Mill by a ford (right).

Go ahead through the kissing gate. The way soon bears half left up the side of the valley with buildings to the left. The way leads to the main road. Go right for a short distance to pass two gateways to residences before going right on a rough track leading back down towards the River Itchen. After a gateway go through the tunnel under the M3. At the far end, before a gate, go sharp left to find a kissing gate. The path follows a field boundary (right). After another kissing gate keep ahead to a kissing gate at Easton Lane. Opposite is Newbridge Cottage.

Keep forward. Before the bottom of a wood there is a kissing gate. Just before the path starts to run into a dip on the edge of **Martyr Worthy**, go left up a wide grass path. Look for a kissing gate on the right to follow a narrow path past the manor house garden (left) to reach the church. This is a Swithun dedication with a 12th-century nave and Norman doorways.

Cross Church Lane to walk up by the side of the church hall (left). On the village edge go through a kissing gate and ahead across a meadow. Later, the path is up against a hedge (left). There are two kissing gates after which thethe path is enclosed. At the far corner, under trees, bear right down a narrow path leading to **Chilland**.

The river and mill are to the right, but to continue on the Pilgrims' Way go left for only a few yards to find hidden steps on the right. Go up the steps to a path which at first follows a high wall (right). At the far end a kissing gate leads to a field. The way is ahead as the path runs gently uphill and slightly half left away from the river

Only stay on the main road for the pub and bus stop at the present Post Office.

STAGE 1 – WINCHESTER TO ALRESFORD

Martyr Worthy church door

(right). Go through a kissing gate. ▶ Keep forward past two houses (left). Go directly ahead across an avenue. The path runs past several houses (left) and joins a track to reach the church lychgate (right) in **Itchen Abbas**.

Here there is a view down to the river.

The church in **Itchen Abbas**, unusual in having fitted carpet, is mainly Victorian but with an original Norman doorway and chancel arch. The river here is said to have provided the inspiration for Charles Kingsley's *The Water Babies*. Foreign Secretary Sir Edward Grey fished here the day before he saw the 'lights going out all over Europe' as World War I was declared in August 1914. The Plough pub on the main road was for some years called the Trout Inn but has seats outside marked The Ship Inn.

Turn right along the road to pass the churchyard (right). The road runs over a millstream and the River Itchen to pass Avington Park gates (right). The mansion of Avington Park can be seen (right) before the junction ahead.

Charles II's mistress Nell Gwynne stayed at the mansion at **Avington Park** after her presence was objected to in the Winchester Cathedral precinct. Later the Prince Regent brought Mrs Fitzherbert to stay. After the death in 1822 of poet Percy Bysshe Shelley his family moved to the grand house for the rest of the century. The Georgian church includes a monument to the poet's brother. The house is open Sundays, Bank Holidays, August Mondays May–September; 2.30pm to 5pm; there is an admission charge.

Go left and after a short distance turn right into Avington Park Golf Club entrance. (Here on the right is a path running into Avington

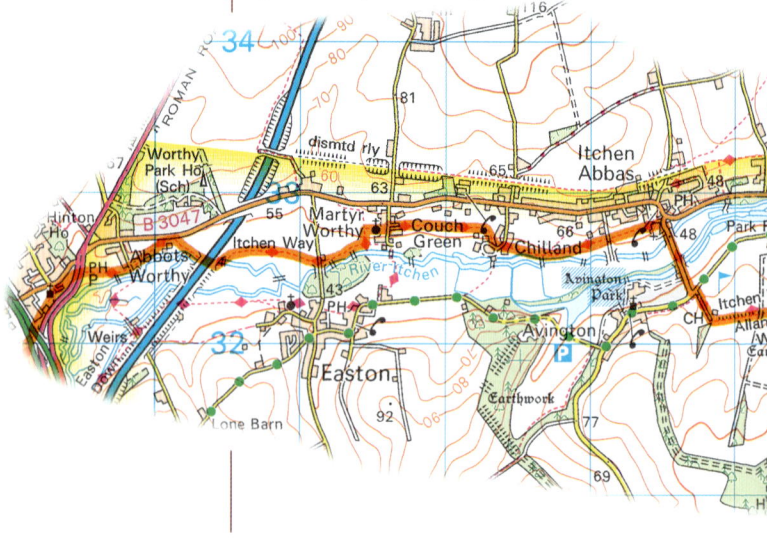

STAGE 1 – WINCHESTER TO ALRESFORD

starting at a small gate.) The main route continues ahead to the clubhouse. Go left along a track by a car park. After running downhill to a junction the way

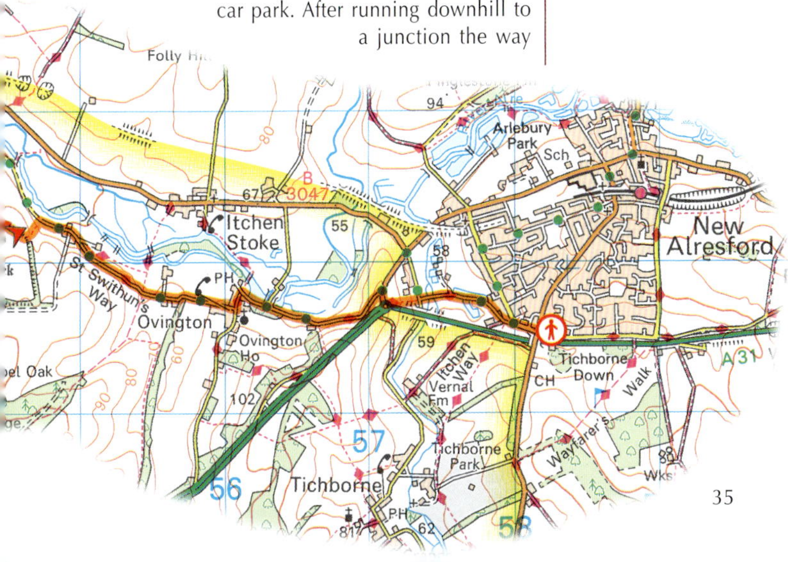

Avington Park

Ovington's old church entrance

continues uphill as a grass way. Beyond a copse, the way bears left down to a stile. Beyond here go half left steeply downhill to a stile at a road.

Turn right on the road to walk past Yavington Farm and uphill towards Ovington. At the top there is a view (left) across the Itchen Valley to Itchen Stoke where its tall church is seen above the houses. As the road rises again there is a view (left) of Lovington House. The road reaches a T-junction in **Ovington**.

> There was a church at **Ovington** in 1284 when the manor was held by the Bishop of Winchester. The much buttressed church, dedicated to St Peter, was completely rebuilt in 1866 leaving the alleged original doorway isolated in the churchyard. The Bush Inn in the village has outlived the forge, bakery and working mill.

Only for the church go right. The way continues left downhill to cross a narrow channel of the Itchen. The

STAGE 1 – WINCHESTER TO ALRESFORD

Bush Inn is to the left. But the route continues to the right on East Lane which occasionally has water on both sides. Having crossed the stream, the lane rises to run high above the valley.

On meeting a main road bear left on a pavement for the crossing point. Once on the far side go half right to find a signpost pointing into the trees. A wooded path rises steeply and soon runs downhill to a road junction. Go ahead on a narrow road which runs through a ford and between watercress beds. On joining another road, Spring Gardens on the edge of **New Alresford**, keep forward past a bus stop to The Cricketers pub at a crossroads.

Only go left along Jacklyns Lane to visit the church and town centre a mile away.

THE PILGRIMS' WAY

STAGE 2
Alresford to Alton

Start	The Cricketers, Alresford
Finish	Alton
Distance	12 miles (19.3km)
Time	5hrs
Maps	OS Explorer OL32 and OL33; Landranger 185 and 186
Refreshments	Pubs at Alresford and Alton; shop at Ropley; cafe at Four Marks and tea shop at Chawton
Public transport	Railway station at Alton; bus at Alresford and Four Marks
Accommodation	Alresford and Four Marks

The way avoids Alresford town centre to head for the even older Bishop's Sutton where church and inn stand together ready to welcome pilgrims and walkers. This contrasts with the next village, pretty Ropley, where the last pub has closed, leaving the restored church and Post Office as the community focus. After a surprise cafe on the path outside Four Marks, the route is wooded on the long approach to Chawton where Jane Austen lived.

STAGE 2 – ALRESFORD TO ALTON

ALRESFORD

This is an old sheep town also known for its watercress sold each May. Production began in the 1860s when the crop was sent to London by the railway known as the Watercress Line. Today this is a steam railway also called the Watercress Line. Pork, ale and watercress sausages are available from the butcher in Broad Street. The 15th-century Globe Inn overlooks Old Alresford Pond which the Bishop of Winchester had dug as a reservoir just 20 years after Thomas Becket's assassination. It is fed by the River Alre flowing from nearby Bishop's Sutton. The churchyard has the graves of Napoleonic prisoners.

The PW continues past The Cricketers (left) along a road called **Tichborne Down**. After some new bungalows there are older buildings and cottages. At the far end the road bears left into Sun Lane. At once go right to follow Whitehill Lane which passes a large solar energy plant (left) and rises to afford a view before running down to **Bishop's Sutton**. After a junction go ahead to a main road. Cross over and go right to the centre of the village by The Ship Inn.

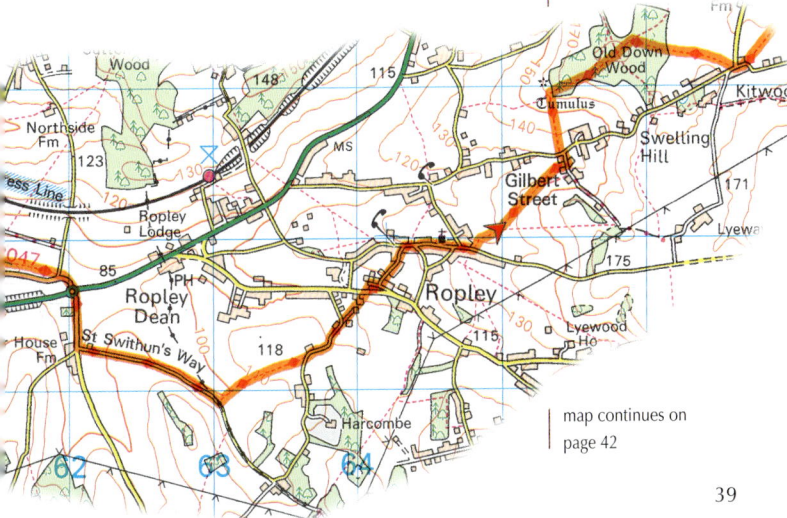

map continues on page 42

BISHOP'S SUTTON

Sutton means south farm and the prefix refers to the Bishop of Winchester's hunting lodge which was here. Its fishponds became today's watercress beds. In about 1150 Bishop Henry de Blois built the church of St Nicholas on a Saxon foundation of Roman brick. The chancel was added in the 13th century. The brick porch, new when future Archbishop William Howley, who crowned Queen Victoria, was vicar, protects rare Norman beakhead decoration. Water and a stamp are available inside for pilgrims. Bruce Blunt, who wrote the carol 'Bethlehem Down' during a moonlit walk between Bishop's Sutton and Ropley, is buried in the churchyard.

Bishop's Sutton milestone: 8 miles from Winchester

Continue past The Ship Inn. Go left by thatched Grove Cottage into Water Lane. Cross the footbridge at the **ford** over the River Alre. When the lane turns sharp left keep ahead into the entrance of Khaya and Fleur-de-lis. Beyond the two houses (left) a path leads to a field. Follow the field boundary (right) beyond which there is a view of the long meadow where the River Alre rises. High up to the left there is sometimes the sight and sound of a steam engine on the **Watercress Line**. The path reaches a gate, where there is a tight gap for walkers (right), leading to Northside Lane.

Go right, to a main road and turn left. At a junction, with a roundabout, the way is ahead, so bear left to find the crossing point on the dual carriageway. On the far side, by a blocked footbridge, bear right to go into Old Park Road.

At a four-way junction go left by a post box to pass a white house (left). The lane at first has a gentle incline. After the road has run downhill and a slight incline look

Path at Kitwood

out for an easily missed set back wooden stile on the left. The path runs half left across a field to a broken stile in a thick field boundary. On the other side go half right (keeping in the same direction) across a second field. On entering a third field there is a clear view (half right) of a large timber frame residence. But the path heads for a white house in the field corner where there is a stile.

Here, on the edge of **Ropley**, go left past Rosemount and along a narrow road which soon runs downhill. At the bend do not go left but turn right into New Barn Farm. At once go left on the track signed Byways. On approaching the house keep forward on a very narrow path. At a road go right for only a few yards to find a metalled but narrow path on the left. At a junction go right to pass thatched Fairway. Turn left up narrow Hammonds Lane. At the top turn right to pass The Forge (right), the shop and church.

According to a survey, **Ropley** is one of England's 25 most idyllic villages, although the pubs have closed. The church, dating from around 1200, is restored after a 2014 fire and open 9am–5pm with tea and coffee available. Opposite the church is Pond Stores and Post Office.

Continue through the village and just beyond Town Farmhouse (left) turn left between a cottage and a pond. The short path leads to a kissing gate. Continue downhill by a fence to a second kissing gate. Go across the next field to a point just right of the large tree. Go through the kissing gate

Walk half left across the field to the corner and beyond the gateway continue in the same direction to a wooden stile. Still keeping in the same direction, or half right from the stile, go over the brow with a solitary house in the distance. At the bottom of the hill cross two stiles in a field corner. Walk half left to a stile in the middle of a fence and on to a stile by a gate at Andrew's Lane.

Turn left to pass Eleanor House with its post box. Here at a road junction go ahead over two stiles. Keep forward uphill along a field boundary (right). Halfway up cross another stile. At the top cross a stile

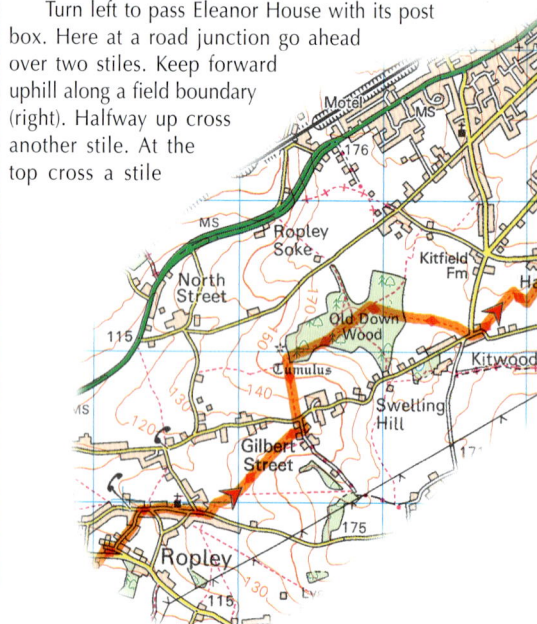

STAGE 2 – ALRESFORD TO ALTON

and go up a slope to the edge of **Old Down Wood**. Continue ahead up the

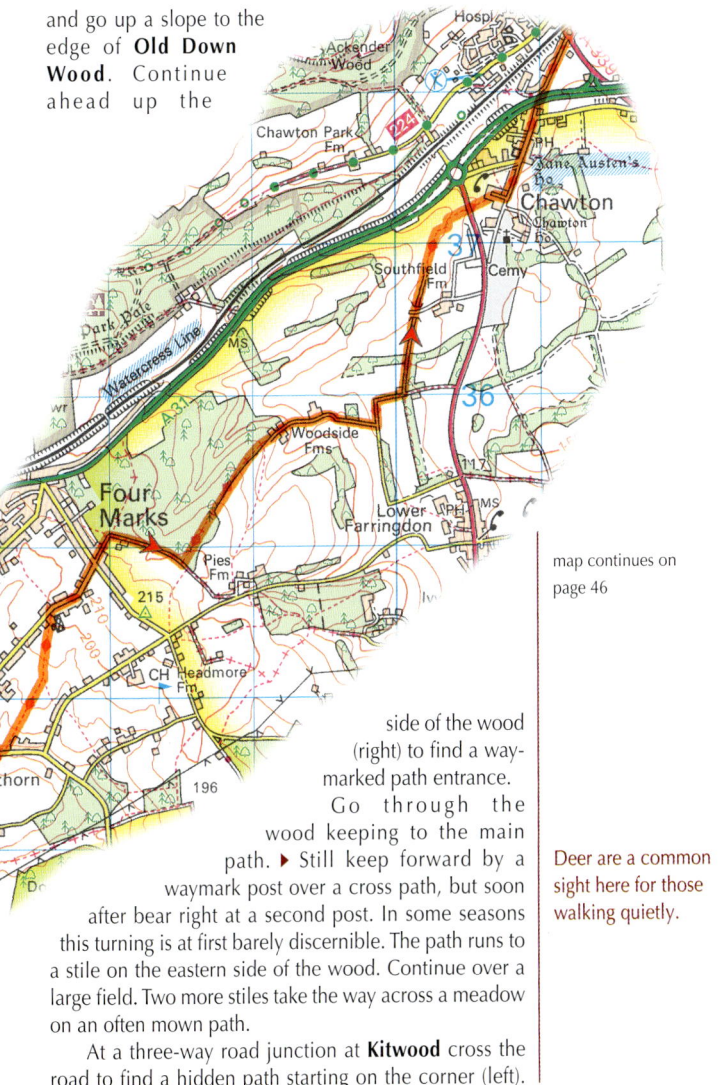

map continues on page 46

side of the wood (right) to find a waymarked path entrance. Go through the wood keeping to the main path. ▶ Still keep forward by a waymark post over a cross path, but soon after bear right at a second post. In some seasons this turning is at first barely discernible. The path runs to a stile on the eastern side of the wood. Continue over a large field. Two more stiles take the way across a meadow on an often mown path.

At a three-way road junction at **Kitwood** cross the road to find a hidden path starting on the corner (left).

Deer are a common sight here for those walking quietly.

The footpath is alongside a high fence (left) and briefly parallel to Kitwood Lane (right). Go through a steel kissing gate. Follow the long field ahead which is part of Homestead Farm. Soon there is a redundant stile (right). At the far end where there are several paths go right, between a redundant stile (left) and kissing gate (right) to walk along another wide grass way. This soon turns left (north-east) to run downhill. Keep going beyond a kissing gate to find another one in a corner at the bottom of the field.

Cross a road to a further kissing gate. Now follow an enclosed narrow path which soon turns left to run uphill past several fields. At the end cross a stile at a track and turn left. Go through a kissing gate and along the side of a field (left) to another kissing gate leading into the back of a garden centre. Soon the path is alongside Tree House Coffee Shop (right).

At the Garthowen Garden Centre main entrance, only cross the road and go ahead if wishing to reach the centre of **Four Marks** and the bus stop.

The Pilgrims' Way continues to the right along the wide road. At a junction keep forward by a post box into Weathermore Lane which runs into woodland. At the first junction go right. After Weathermore Cottage (right) the track runs just inside the woodland. At the end of the trees go left to stay just inside the eastern side. This track in New Copse emerges from the trees at a viewpoint and hamlet to become Woodside Lane.

After Lower Woodside Farm, at the bottom of the hill where the road bends right, turn left along a rough lane. At a junction go right with the main path over open ground. The way runs under oaks to a four-way junction by Park Cottage. Before the house go left past a barn. A wide woodland way runs ahead and passes under a bridge. At the end continue on a narrow path. This bears right, downhill, and left to go through a copse. On the northern side turn right, down an enclosed path to a kissing gate and steps. Cross a main road and go up steps to a stile. An enclosed path runs to a short residential road at **Chawton**.

CHAWTON

The Greyfriar pub dates from the 16th century. Jane Austen lived in Chawton (Jane Austen's House is open most days and has an admission charge) for the last eight years of her life until 1817 thanks to her brother inheriting the Elizabethan manor house. She was given the choice of this house or one on the Godmersham estate (see Stage 14). The tea shop opposite Jane Austen's house is called Cassandra's Cup, after Jane's sister who in 1804 became the first person to mention 'afternoon tea' in writing. Cassandra is buried in the churchyard. Following a fire, the church was rebuilt in 1872 to a design by Sir Arthur Blomfield. Among the books written here by Jane Austen is *Mansfield Park* which she read aloud in draft to her brother Henry, the curate, during a carriage ride to London.

Approaching Chawton

Go ahead to the village street where there is a seat overlooking parkland. Only go right to visit the church beyond a row of cottages.

Continue left through the village centre. Walk ahead past **Jane Austen's House** (left) and The Greyfriar (right).

THE PILGRIMS' WAY

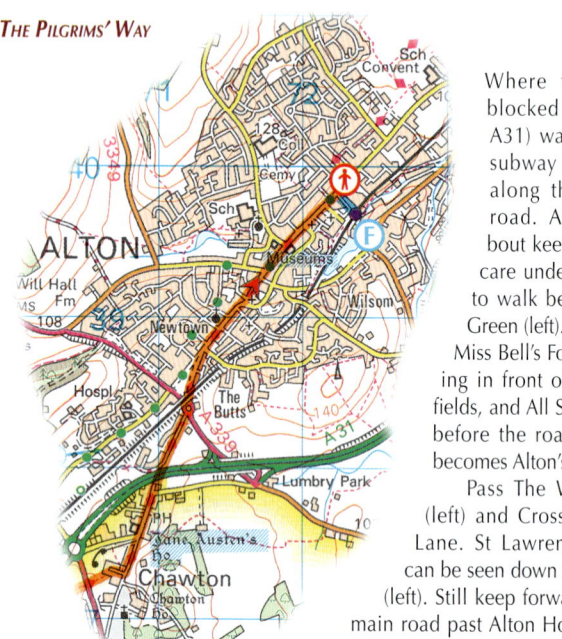

Where the road is blocked (due to the A31) walk through a subway to continue along the old main road. At a roundabout keep ahead with care under the railway to walk beside Lincoln Green (left). Later there is Miss Bell's Fountain standing in front of former hop fields, and All Saints Church, before the road eventually becomes Alton's High Street. Pass The White Horse (left) and Cross and Pillory Lane. St Lawrence's Church can be seen down Church Street (left). Still keep forward along the main road past Alton House Hotel to reach the station. Station Road is opposite The Railway Arms but for a short cut go right by the crucifix down Paper Mill Lane.

STAGE 3
Alton to Farnham

Start	Alton
Finish	Farnham
Distance	11 miles (17.7km)
Time	5hrs
Maps	OS Explorer 144 and 145; Landranger 186
Refreshments	Pubs at Alton, Upper Froyle, Lower Froyle, Bentley and Farnham
Public transport	Railway stations at Alton and Farnham; bus at Bentley
Accommodation	Alton

This was, like Kent, hop country and there are sometimes hop kilns to be seen. Holybourne, Froyle and Bentley are claimed to be on the Pilgrims' Way. However, the original route into Farnham is uncertain. Today the main road has an unbearable amount of traffic and so some follow the footpath alongside the railway. The old route may have gone north from Bentley towards Crondall where there was a castle once belonging to the Bishop of Winchester. This guide stays on the understood route out of Bentley, briefly ignoring the St Swithun's Way on its diversion, and then takes to higher ground to enter Farnham by way of the Bishop Fox Steps alongside Farnham Castle.

From Alton station
Bear right along Station Road to pass Waitrose, and at Anstey Road (150 yards/0.1km) turn right.

In Anstey Road pass The Railway Arms (left) and go left up Nursery Road. Between the row of garages and the bus stop on the right go right, down a long path. The way runs in a straight line over two roads. Keep ahead down the road opposite and where it bends right, keep ahead up an enclosed way. At another road cross over to enter a large playing field.

The Pilgrims' Way

ALTON

St Lawrence's Church, which belonged to Winchester's Hyde Abbey, has rare early Norman arches. The double-nave church still bears marks of a 1643 Civil War skirmish. Until 2015 Alton was a brewing town where St John Henry Newman's father was a brewery manager from 1816 to 1819 during his son's teenage years. The Town Hall, at the top of Cross and Pillory Lane, was the scene in 1867 of the murder hearing following the discovery of 'Sweet' Fanny Adams' body in a hop field. The local history Curtis Museum was founded in 1856 by Jane Austen's doctor, William Curtis. Curtis was a relative of botanist William Curtis (1746–1799) who had served his apprenticeship in Alton. The railway station, now the terminus for both the main line and Watercress Line, opened as a through route to Winchester in 1865.

The infant River Wey at Alton

Walkers scrunch over conkers here in the autumn.

In the middle cross a school access road and still keep forward towards a chestnut tree. ◀ Go through a gap ahead and turn left on an enclosed path by Eggar's School. At a junction go right, along a tunnel of trees. Continue over a pedestrian crossing in Treloar College

STAGE 3 – ALTON TO FARNHAM

grounds. The path soon runs between high fences to a road at **Holybourne**. Go left to pass a long, converted 17th-century barn and right at a junction by Howards Farm. The road passes the church (right).

> Holy Rood church in **Holybourne** has a Norman tower and a 13th-century chancel. The ancient building hides the village pond fed by the 'holy bourne' which rises here and feeds the River Wey. Church Cottage, at the start of Church Lane, dates from the 15th century. The lane leads to the village centre and The Lawn, home of novelist Elizabeth Gaskell who died there in 1865.

Beyond the church go ahead along an enclosed path and past a stone building. The way bends round to a junction. Go left down a tunnel of trees and along the side (right) of a field. Continue ahead over a large field and across a bridleway running through a belt of trees. Then still go forward over another field. On the far side go up a wooded slope and ahead along the side (left) of a field. Half right can be seen the buildings of **Bonham's Farm**.

map continues on page 50

The Pilgrims' Way

Soon there is a handy log seat facing the view before the path has an arboretum to the left.

The path runs gently down to briefly join a track at a double bend. Go forward but now with a field boundary to the right. ◄ In the corner of the field take the right-hand path to another field. The way is ahead across the field to pass just to the right of a pylon. On entering a smaller field follow its side (left).

At the bottom the way is enclosed just as there is a glimpse of a lake (right). The now deeply wooded path climbs up to the start of a road. Follow the road ahead past houses, a large garage and farm buildings to enter **Upper Froyle**.

UPPER FROYLE

The church's rare dedication to The Assumption is due to its early association with Winchester's St Mary's Abbey which owned the manor. The church, dating from the 13th century, was greatly enhanced by 19th-century lord of the manor Sir Hubert Miller who also lived in Venice. Among the items he brought back were vestments, one of which is usually displayed. A new window depicts both Winchester Cathedral and Canterbury Cathedral to acknowledge that the village is on the Pilgrims' Way. Sir Hubert was responsible for the small statues of saints attached to the estate houses. The high street walls were built by Napoleonic prisoners.

After the small green by Gothic Cottage (left) only turn right for the Hen and Chicken pub.

The Way continues ahead past early 19th-century Froyle House (left) and a high stone wall (right). Beyond the church there is a long low wall (right). Where this ends, and before Fern

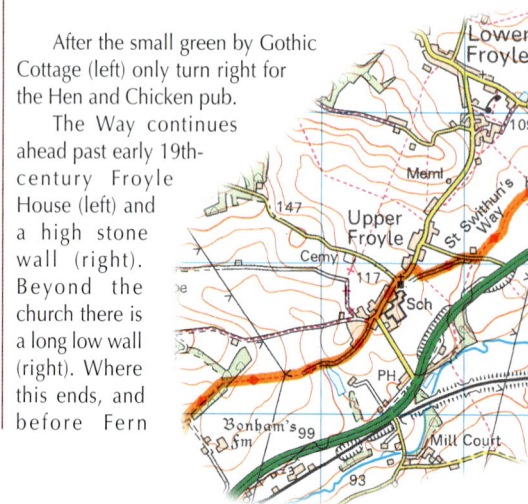

50

STAGE 3 – ALTON TO FARNHAM

Cottage, go right, over a stile. Keep over the grass to pass near an oak tree (right) to a kissing gate. Turn left on the Froyle Park driveway. On joining a road keep forward for a short distance before turning left through a kissing gate.

Follow the field boundary (right). After another gate there is a dip as the way enters the next field. Bear right, into the trees where a wooden bridge crosses a stream. Now follow the long hawthorn hedge (left) to reach a road in **Lower Froyle**. To the left is The Anchor pub.

map continues on page 54

Turn right along the road, and at Sycamore Cottage (left) go left up a track signed **Coldrey** and which is part of the original Pilgrims' Way. Beyond the

> The Georgian front hides an Elizabethan building.

houses (left) are the Coldrey Farm buildings. While the track turns right down an avenue keep forward through a kissing gate by a wide gateway. The path runs downhill to join a driveway from Coldrey House. ◄ As the driveway curves to the right again keep forward through a gap by a gateway. Just inside there is a view (left) along an old stone wall.

The way forward is a short wooded causeway with the water hardly discernible on either side. Go through the kissing gate and ahead up a slope to the brow. Head for the left side of the house ahead. Once alongside the house keep forward to a stile in the corner of the field. Turn left up the drive to **Pax Hill**.

> The house at **Pax Hill** was the home of Scouts founder Robert Baden-Powell. After he died his wife Olave gave the house to the Girl Guides as a training centre. It is now a care home. Until almost the end of the 20th century hops were still grown in the field south of the house and now two fields have become a vineyard.

Just before the drive turns right go right, onto a footpath. The straight wooded path runs to a kissing gate. The way is now alongside paddocks as it runs ahead. Bear left and after a few yards go right. The path is alongside a field boundary (right). Pass into a second field. On the far side of a hedge (right) is the vineyard. The path runs up to a farm gate and through a small field. After a smaller gate the path is past a long row of cottages at **Jenkyn Place** in Bentley.

At a road in **Bentley** turn right and then left into Church Lane. The church is at the end of the road. At the church the road turns right in front of Church Cottage (with post box). Pass Well Cottage (left). At the bottom of the road turn left into Hole Lane. ◄

> At the next junction only go right down School Lane, and right at a turning marked 'private', to reach the shop, pub and bus stop in the village centre. The Farnham bus stops outside the Post Office but the Alton bus stops at a shelter in the road opposite the Memorial Hall.

The PW continues ahead still on Hole Lane. After a bend the St Swithun's Way leaves the road at a stile (right) while the PW continues on the road. At a junction bear left into the **East Green** road. After a short distance go left

Stage 3 – Alton to Farnham

BENTLEY

The church, standing on the northern edge of the village, has an early Norman chancel and a tower built around 1200. The stone is local Malmstone as used for Winchester's Hyde Abbey. Nearby Well Cottage to the south is a reminder of the claim that pilgrims stopped here to draw water. The yews propped up over the churchyard path may have been growing for at least 350 years. Jane Austen's brother Henry came here from Farnham in 1824 to be perpetual curate. At the western crossroads the village sign, in the form of a giant history book, was designed in 1923 by Robert Baden-Powell who exhibited it at the Scout Jamboree held during the British Empire Exhibition at Wembley.

Bentley churchyard path

up a wide entrance into a wood where the St Swithun's Way rejoins the route.

Beyond a gateway the path runs along the edge of Wallfield Copse before bearing right, through the middle. On the eastern side go right for only a few yards then turn left over a small footbridge. Walk ahead by a hedge (right) but as it turns away keep ahead up over a field. At the top follow a field boundary (left). **Hill Farm** can be seen over to the right.

The Pilgrims' Way

In the corner go through a gap and ahead across a field. A low gate leads to a lane. Turn left past a solar farm (right) and right, up a wide bridleway. The solar panels appear again (right). At Old Farmhouse Lane go right and at once left where the bridleway continues. The way passes from Hampshire into Surrey as it begins running downhill. After rising, another track joins from the left. The way meets a road at Dippenhall Farm.

Go up the road opposite. The route is now metalled for some distance. At the end there is a four-way junction with a Hampshire sign (left). Go ahead on the road which is just inside Surrey as the county boundary runs along the left side. Old Timbers (right) is halfway along the road. As the road bends left keep forward on a metalled estate road which runs downhill.

After a bridge the road climbs steeply past Lower Old Farm and double bends to the top of the hill. Stay on the road past Keepers Cottage and round another double bend. Beyond **Middle Old Park** (left) the hard surface swings left as the PW continues ahead as a rough way. This runs gently downhill and up through woodland. At two cottages (right) go forward on the track. After Park Farm the way reaches a T-junction. Turn right along Old Park Lane.

At the end of a row of cottages (left) there

Farnham Castle

is Grange Farm where a stone barn and a quince tree can be seen. Here the St Swithun's Way turns right to run down to Waitrose in Farnham. But the PW continues ahead to the end of the road. Cross the main road with care to go up steps to a raised pavement. Turn right on the fenced path with **Farnham Castle**'s outer wall on the left to reach its entrance.

> Strategic **Farnham Castle** was begun in 1138 by Bishop Henry de Blois as a halfway house on the Winchester to London road. The Winchester bishops were Farnham's lords of the manor. Bishop Fox's Steps, which lead down Castle Hill, were made in sets of seven steps and seven paces for Bishop Richard Fox who lived here during his last years in the 1520s. King John, Elizabeth I, James I and George III all stayed in the castle, which between 1660 and 1932 became the Bishop of Winchester's principal home. The castle keep can be visited daily and admission is free.

Only to enter the castle go left at the first entrance. Stay on the path beyond the castle entrances to find the way, continuing as Bishop Fox's Steps and leading down from the gatehouse to Castle Street in Farnham. At the bottom of Castle Street go left and at a crossroads right into South Street. Cross Farnham Bypass to reach the bottom of Station Hill. The PW continues to the left with the NDW.

For Farnham station
Walk up Station Hill past The Mulberry (right) and bear right to the station (150 yards/0.1km).

STAGE 4
Farnham to Guildford

Start	Farnham
Finish	St Catherine's village, Guildford
Distance	10½ miles (16.8km)
Time	4hrs
Maps	OS Explorer 145; Landranger 186
Refreshments	Pubs at Farnham, Puttenham and St Catherine's; tea rooms at Seale (Tuesday–Sunday) and Watts Gallery
Toilets	Seale
Public transport	Railway stations at Farnham and Guildford; bus at St Catherine's village
Accommodation	Farnham and Puttenham

The Pilgrims' Way now leaves behind the St Swithun's Way and often finds its ancient route being shared with the North Downs Way. The way out of Farnham is also the NDW but soon there is the first of many partings of the ways as a more authentic route is rediscovered. Here are encountered the sandy, or greensand, path surfaces which will become familiar across Surrey. This section has one of the best cafes on the PW with the Watts Gallery at Compton being perfectly placed by the path. Afterwards the path is above Loseley before approaching the ancient chapel at St Catherine's outside Guildford.

From Farnham station
Walk down Station Hill passing The Mulberry to the dual carriageway (150 yards/0.1km). The NDW starting point is to the right.

At the bottom of Station Hill turn east along Farnham Bypass keeping the traffic to the left. At once pass an artwork (right) erected in 2015 to mark the start of the North Downs Way.

The Pilgrims' Way

FARNHAM

St Andrew's, Farnham's parish church

Farnham is an old market town. Radical pamphleteer and *Rural Rides* author William Cobbett was a young gardener at the castle. His birthplace in 1763 is now The William Cobbett pub in Bridge Street and he is buried outside the 12th-century St Andrew's Church. He visited other stretches of the Pilgrims' Way and in his writings took the view that the Reformation had been disastrous for England. Jane Austen's brother Henry was curate here for two years from 1822 before moving to Bentley. The Old Vicarage in the churchyard was built in 1418 by the future Bishop of Winchester Henry Beaufort. Farnham Maltings recalls the town's lost brewing heritage. The museum in West Street was the home of an 18th-century maltster and hop merchant. Hops were once grown behind The Hop Blossom pub in Long Garden Way off Castle Street.

After a short distance leave the traffic by going right, into a lane which bears left through trees. Go right at a junction. Soon there is a gate (left) leading to Wild Bean Cafe. Later the lane is alongside the River Wey (left). Pass Snayleslynch Farm and on approaching The Kilns bear right to go under a railway bridge.

Stage 4 – Farnham to Guildford

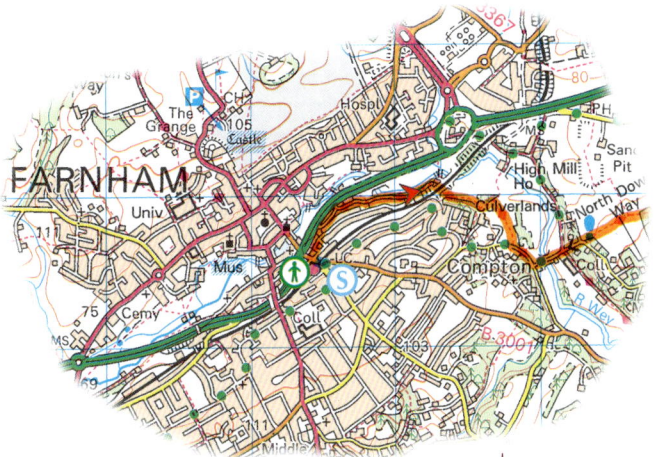

map continues on page 60

An enclosed way runs ahead alongside a wood (right) and a water meadow with High Mill House in the distance. At a T-junction go left for a short distance then turn right through a gate. Here there is a carved wooden seat. Follow the wooded path to a kissing gate at a road. Go left along the road which is on the side of a hill. Round the corner go left into Moor Park Lane. Cross the River Wey and pass The Walled Garden and the entrance to **Moor Park House** (right).

> In the 14th century the owner of **Moor Park House** was the Bishop of Winchester. A 1630 building here was bought in the 1680s by Sir William Temple who laid out magnificent gardens and employed Jonathan Swift as secretary. A public footpath runs from the gates past the now mostly 18th-century house.

Walk up the steep hill ahead, but at the top, as the road bears right, go left on a footpath which turns sharply. Beyond a kissing gate the way is along the side of a meadow. At the far end go through a gate to enter

The Pilgrims' Way

Runfold Wood. On the far side the path runs down steps to a cross path. Turn left. There is soon a field on the right.

At a road turn right. Cross the road with care at a double bend. By the side of number 9 (left) go between barriers to follow a narrow path. ◄ The way meets a road by a bus stop in **Runfold**.

To the left is the former Jolly Farmer pub. Go right, along the main road, Guildford Road, which is on the line of the Pilgrims' Way. Hop Cottage is to the left. A path runs on the right side. Where the road divides at Whiteway's Fork (which 19th-century guide writer, Julia Cartwright, calls 'Whiteways End') the main traffic goes left up the Hog's Back. Meanwhile, the PW continues ahead past Whiteways Cottage (right) and along Seale Lane.

The path is now on the left but after the Blighton Lane junction switches back to the right. A bungalow on the right is called Pilgrims Cottage. The Thundery Hill crossroads, where there is a seat, is known as **Sandy Cross**. Where the path ends there is soon another on the left, after the 40 mph sign. Continue to the junction in **Seale**. Cross the road to pass the post box and enter Wood Lane. Pass Manor Farm Craft Centre and tea room (right).

Occasionally there is a view through the trees (left) to a lake. In autumn apples and conkers may be found lying on the path.

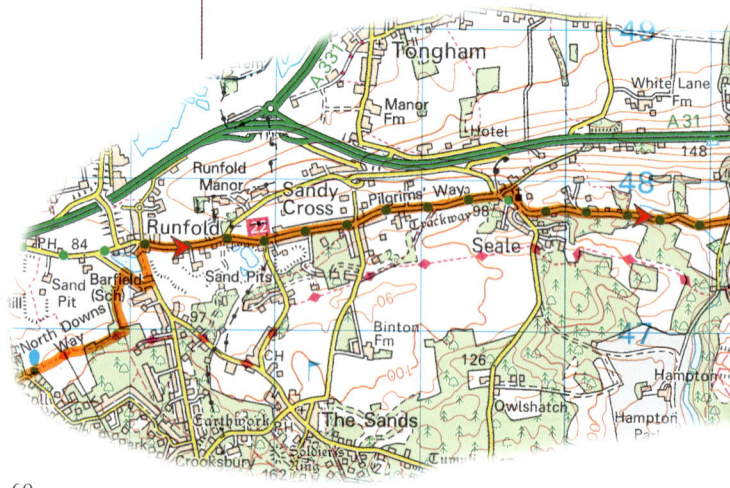

STAGE 4 – FARNHAM TO GUILDFORD

In 1487 the village of **Seale** was called Zeyle. The church dates from the 12th century having been built by Waverley Abbey which is to the

Seale church porch

map continues on page 64

south-west on the River Wey. The church's largest bell came from Chertsey Abbey at the dissolution of the monasteries. Eastend Farm is 16th-century. According to Cartwright the road through Seale was grass as late as the end of Victoria's reign.

Just beyond the farm building, and level with Pilgrim Cottages (left), go right, down steps and follow the path past the farmyard and through a gate into the churchyard. The path runs up the sloping ground to pass toilets and reach the lychgate.

Go through the lychgate and left past the war memorial. Take the Puttenham Road (left). There is briefly a path on the left as the road curves. Pass Eastend Farm (left). After a double bend, known as Beggar's Corner, there is a wide grass verge (right). At the Totford Lane crossroads the road becomes Seale Lane. There is a path on the grass to the left as far as a terrace of three cottages. Round a double bend is a view of Shoelands which dates from 1616.

Stay on the winding road which soon starts to climb up towards **Puttenham** with a view of its hop fields. On entering the old village at a bend, the road becomes just The Street as it runs gently downhill with a view of the Puttenham church high up ahead.

> The Puttenham church porch doorway dates from around 1170 so is as old as Becket's murder. The nave is 12th-century while the tower was added in the early Tudor period. The lectern features the Winchester shield. Outside the west end there is a well. The PW originally ran past the porch rather than following the line of today's road.

To reach the stop for Farnham buses go up School Lane (left) which climbs the Hog's Back. At a divide go left and along a field at the side of the main road (right). Beyond a gate and a cafe garden is the bus stop (1 mile/1.6km). ◂

Bus drivers should be hailed to ensure the bus pulls into the lay-by.

The PW continues along the village street past The Good Intent pub (left) and uphill to pass the church

STAGE 4 – FARNHAM TO GUILDFORD

Hops at Puttenham

(right). At the main road go right, past the gateway to a house called Puttenham Priory and along a high path to reach The Pickled Pig, the former Jolly Farmer. Here the PW once emerged from the right. Go left, crossing the road, pass the pub car park and soon Pilgrims Way Cottage (right).

From the track there are glimpses of a golf course. Eggs are often for sale outside Clear Barn Farm (left). Pass a turning to Greyfriars Vineyard (left). After Monks Grove Farm do not bear right but keep ahead downhill and alongside the lawn of a house called Questors. The path becomes sandy. Ignore all turnings and keep forward on the now wooded path. At a metalled road leading to Monkshatch (left) go right to pass under two bridges. ▶

The second bridge is the old main road crossing built in 1931 to a design by Edwin Lutyens who added two crosses to mark the PW.

At a junction, only go right to visit the Compton chapel and, a little further on, the parish church in the village.

> St Nicholas Church in **Compton** is mainly Norman, with a Saxon tower and chancel arch, a very rare double-deck chancel and an anchorite's cell. The Watts Chapel in the nearby cemetery was designed

in the 1890s by Mary Watts using a fusion of styles, including art nouveau, Romanesque and Egyptian, to produce in Surrey a version of the Church of the Holy Sepulchre in Jerusalem.

The PW does not pass through the village centre but turns left and after a very short distance right to pass a pond (left). By the post box is the entrance to Watts Gallery and tea shop.

The **Watts Gallery and artists' village** is a development begun by artist GF Watts (1817–1904) and continued by his wife Mary (1849–1938) whose individual studios can be viewed. Mary's pottery showroom, opened in 1901, is now the tea shop, noted for its unique rarebit and also serving Loseley ice cream first produced with Jersey milk from nearby Loseley Park in 1968.

The very sandy track runs gently uphill past Watts Gallery (left). Where the track swings right at farm buildings keep ahead on the narrow path. The PW becomes a long hollow way as it rises through woodland. Beyond a cross path the way ahead continues to rise but later drops down. Trees to the right are part of the Loseley Estate's nature reserve. A wide ride in the trees (right) has a gated path leading to **Loseley House**.

The More-Molyneux family has been resident for five centuries at **Loseley House** situated in Loseley Park. The house was rebuilt in the 1560s after Elizabeth I declared it 'inadequate' for her lengthy visit. Reused stone for the work came from the just closed Waverley Abbey. James I also stayed there. Loseley, with its walled garden and dairy farm buildings, has often featured in films.

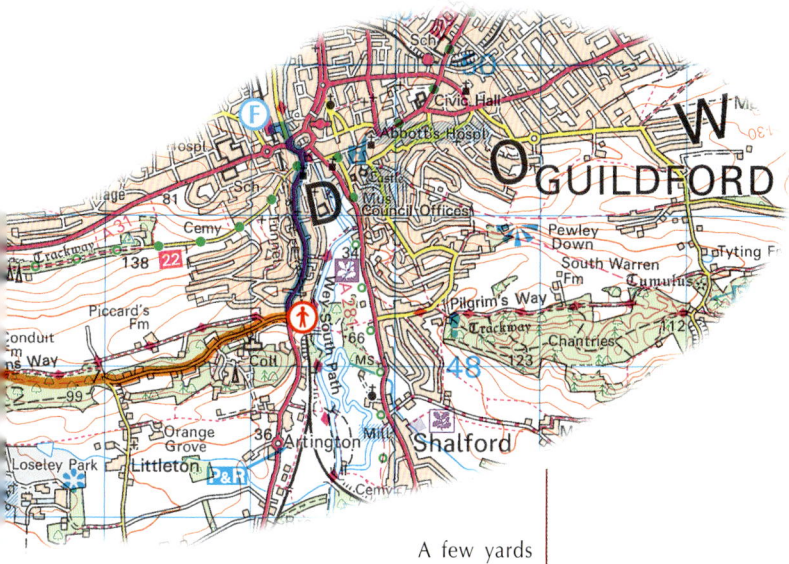

A few yards ahead the path divides, with the NDW taking the left-hand fork. The PW continues straight ahead just inside the woodland. At the far end the path runs downhill to a lane at a point known as Littleton Cross.

Bear right and at once left up Sandy Lane. The odd isolated houses have such names as Pilgrim Wood, Pilgrim Gardens and Bothy. After passing the Surrey Police HQ entrance (right), the lane runs downhill. Later there is a pavement on the right by the wall of Brabhoeuf Manor. The NDW joins from the left before Sandy Lane reaches Portsmouth Road at St Catherine's village on the edge of Guildford. Ahead is Ye Olde Ship Inn.

For Guildford station

Turn left opposite the pub to pass a bus stop. At the bottom of the hill stay on the left side of the road to reach the station (1 mile/1.6km).

The Pilgrims' Way

STAGE 5
Guildford to Box Hill

Start	St Catherine's village, Guildford
Finish	Westhumble, Box Hill
Distance	13½ miles (21.7km)
Time	6hrs
Maps	OS Explorer 145 and 146; Landranger 186 and 187
Refreshments	Pubs at St Catherine's, Shere, Gomshall and Westhumble; tea shops at Abinger Hammer and Denbies
Public transport	Railway stations at Guildford, Gomshall and Westhumble (Box Hill & Westhumble station)
Accommodation	Guildford and Shere

The route is common with the NDW as far as dramatic St Martha's Hill. Soon after, the PW passes through the Surrey villages of Shere and Gomshall, and Abinger Hammer where the old post office is now an all day tea room for walkers. After here the authentic route has been much disputed but the consensus now is that it should run north of the railway on much the same course as the NDW. The entry to the Mole Valley is by way of the vineyard north of Dorking to be in line for the Box Hill stepping stones.

From Guildford station
Turn right out of the station's main entrance. At the road junction cross the end of Farnham Road (right) and keep forward on a pavement leading to Portsmouth Road which runs uphill to Ye Olde Ship Inn (1 mile/1.6km). There is a bus stop at the start of the hill.

Pass the 17th-century Ye Olde Ship Inn (left) and after a few yards turn left into Ferry Lane. Only to visit St Catherine's Chapel, at once go half right up the steep grass path running under oak trees. Avoid the track signed 'Unsuitable for motor vehicles'.

GUILDFORD

Guildford is the county town of Surrey where William the Conqueror built the castle to guard the gap in the ridge. The landmark cathedral, designed by Edward Maufe, was built between 1936 and 1961 after the Guildford Diocese had been carved out of the giant Winchester Diocese in 1927. Holy Trinity, which briefly served as the cathedral, has the tomb of Archbishop George Abbot (1562–1633) who founded the Oxbridge-style Abbot's Hospital almshouses opposite. Cow & Gate started next door in 1885 when grocers Charles and Leonard Gates, who joined the temperance movement, poured the wines and spirits stock into the gutter to concentrate on dairy products. Also in the High Street are the 14th-century Guildhall with its projecting clock added in 1683, and the Angel Hotel where the London to Portsmouth stagecoach stopped before climbing the hill and passing St Catherine's Chapel.

ST CATHERINE'S

The village around Braboeuf Manor, occupied by The University of Law, takes its name from the hilltop chapel. The manor's name is derived from the Norman family de Braboeuf who held the manor from 1232 to 1362. In 1171 it had been part of the larger Artington Manor granted by Henry II to lawyer 'Master David of London' as reward for diplomatic services in Rome following Becket's murder. David soon passed the manor to Ranulf (or Ralph) de Broc, who had helped Becket's assassins.

St Catherine's Chapel

St Catherine's Chapel was built around 1317 as a chapel of ease for St Nicholas Church at the bottom of the hill in Guildford. The size of the chapel doorways indicates that there were large numbers of visitors. The building was abandoned at the Reformation and had become derelict by the time JWM Turner sketched it at the end of the 18th century. He came by boat up the River Wey and also painted the St Catherine's Fair which was held here each September around St Matthew's Day from 1308 until World War I.

THE PILGRIMS' WAY

> The crossing was a ford until succeeded in the 1750s by a ferry which ran until 1963. The replacement bridge was built in 1978.

The PW continues down Ferry Lane to cross the railway and pass Pilgrim Cottage (left) and Ferry Cottage – once a tea room – to reach the River Wey. The river was canalised as the Godalming Navigation in 1764 with barges able to reach London using the Wey Navigation and the Thames. ◄

Go right, along the towpath and cross the footbridge. On the far side keep ahead downstream for a short distance before turning inland across a reed bed. Just before a small footbridge there is a view back to St Catherine's Chapel on the hill. Continue ahead across a field and through a gateway into Shalford Park. A path runs half left across usually mown grass to a gateway at a road.

> Number 5, Priors Field (left), has metal gates featuring the PW by local artist and blacksmith Terrence Clark.

Cross over to go ahead up a road called Pilgrims Way. ◄ Where the road becomes Echo Pit Road and houses on the right end, go half right on a path marked Chantry Wood.

At a cross path keep ahead past a cottage (right) and up a wide wooded track. The way runs up and down with later a view (left) of **Pewley Down**. Where the wide path swings left to **South Warren Farm** keep forward. Soon the path is very sandy as it runs between paddocks before plunging into an often dark wood.

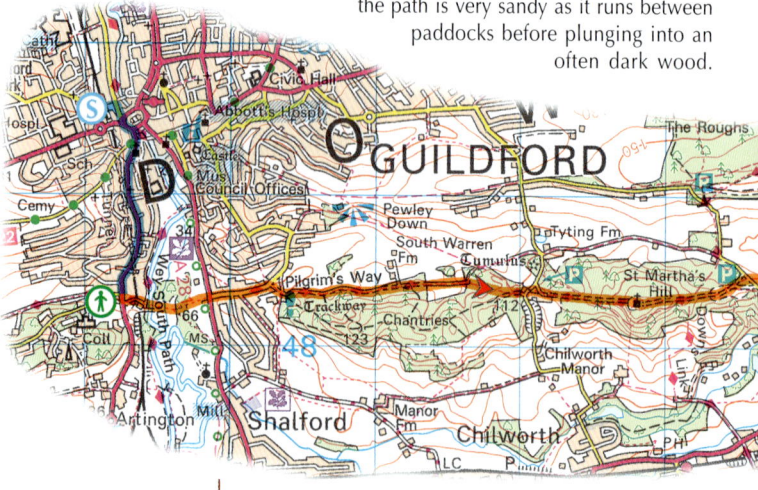

STAGE 5 – GUILDFORD TO BOX HILL

On meeting Halfpenny Lane, on a difficult hill bend, go left for a few yards and then right by Southern Way Cottage.

A steep path runs uphill to cross a drive by thatched St Martha's Priory (right), a 1932 Arts and Crafts house. A sandy path runs ahead.

River Wey bridge below St Catherine's Chapel

map continues on page 72

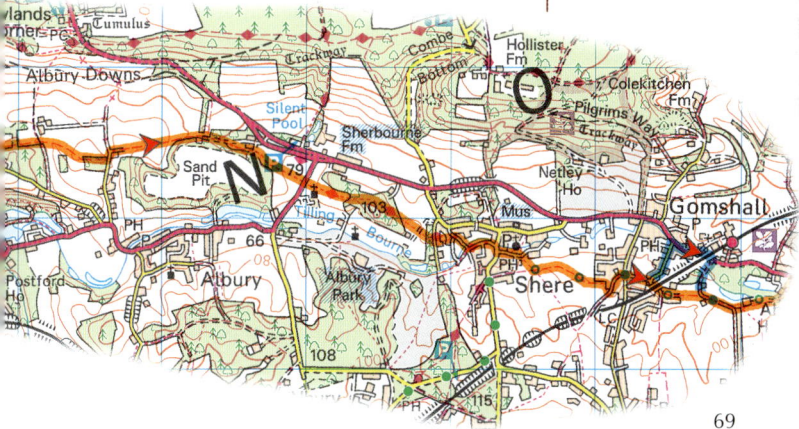

The Pilgrims' Way

Follow this as it enters woodland. Ignore any turning and keep on the main rising path to reach St Martha's Church at a viewpoint on **St Martha's Hill**.

ST MARTHA'S HILL

Sometimes called Martyr's Hill after Thomas Becket, the hill rises 570 feet above sea level giving a view of seven counties. The trees are planted to anchor the greensand soil. St Martha's Church, dating from about 1100, had a Becket chapel and now, after an 1850 restoration, there is a modern depiction of the saint in a window. Marks scratched in stonework are claimed as pilgrim crosses. The dedication to Lazarus's sister Martha is rare. The church appears in Kenneth Branagh's film *In the Bleak Midwinter* and the hill features in the opening sequence of the 1944 film *A Canterbury Tale* when costumed characters are seen riding up the path. French actress Yvonne Arnaud, who lived in Guildford where the theatre has her name, is commemorated by the churchyard's east gate.

Walk through the churchyard and on the far side follow the sandy path which soon veers slightly to the right to go downhill. The track continues through woodland where the NDW swings away to the left. A few yards on there is a Downs Link stone (right) and then a wartime pill box (left). Soon the path runs on two sides of an oak tree to reach a junction. Bull posts mark the way.

Take the main path half left by a waymark post. As the narrow bridleway approaches a car park follow the way round to the right to meet a road. By the oak tree opposite take the path which follows a fence (left). Soon there is a hedge (right) before the path is alongside a wood. The path runs downhill to cross a footpath and enter a field. Go half right up the sandy field to enter a wood to turn left. At the end the path falls very steeply down to Water Lane by half-hidden Water Lane Cottages. Go left and almost at once right into another lane which soon passes garages then narrows before a gate.

A long path runs gently uphill to woodland where there is a cottage called Timbercroft (right). Continue ahead, but after a short distance turn half right off the

STAGE 5 – GUILDFORD TO BOX HILL

main track onto a footpath. The narrow way runs through trees. Soon to the left there is a worksite. With care, walk over a plant-crossing track. The footpath enters more trees and bears right. The short path leads to a stile where there is a sudden view of an impressive church in **Albury Park**.

Follow a fence (left) along a field and at the far end cross another stile to walk over a stream running down from Silent Pool to join the **Tilling Bourne river**. A kissing gate leads to rural Albury Street. Go ahead by the post box and up a slope to a gate and kissing gate at Albury Park.

> The large church at **Albury Park** was built in 1840 for the now defunct Catholic Apostolic Church by Henry Drummond who lived at Albury Park. The following year he closed the ancient Saxon church which has a 15th-century St Christopher wall painting and a chapel remodelled by Pugin. Drummond built a replacement in nearby Albury village. The inn and road through the park, which was probably part of the original Pilgrims' Way, had been closed in 1785. The mansion, Tudor but with many 18th- and 19th-century alterations, passed to the Percy family and is now divided into flats. The old church may be visited via the gateway (on the line of the old road) at the south end of Albury Street (10am–5pm, winter 3pm).

A wide tread can be discerned in the grass ahead as the way crosses a field (with a view back to the church) and follows a boundary (right) to a kissing gate. A deep path runs uphill and soon downhill in a wood hiding the big house to the south. Beyond a gate the path continues ahead in a field and alongside a young woodland (right). After crossing the main drive, the path meets a kissing gate in the corner. A short woodland path runs downhill to a lane in **Shere**. Cross over and take the narrow path ahead which follows a high wall. At another lane, by the Old Rectory (right), go right, downhill, and round a corner to ford the Tilling Bourne. The road on the far side

THE PILGRIMS' WAY

follows a stone wall (left) and passes cottages, including Old Prison House. Soon the river is on the left as the street reaches Shere village centre. The White Horse and The William Bray pubs are to the right.

> **Shere** has been called one of the most beautiful villages in England although, being remote, there are today too many cars in front of the ancient cottages. The church, dating from 1190 and featured in the second Bridget Jones film, is dedicated to St James the Great. Displayed inside is a 13th-century Madonna and Child, just two inches high, which may have fallen from a pilgrim staff. The lychgate was designed in 1902 by Edwin Lutyens who was responsible for several nearby buildings. A natural spring drinking fountain in Middle Street is now dry due to a falling water table.

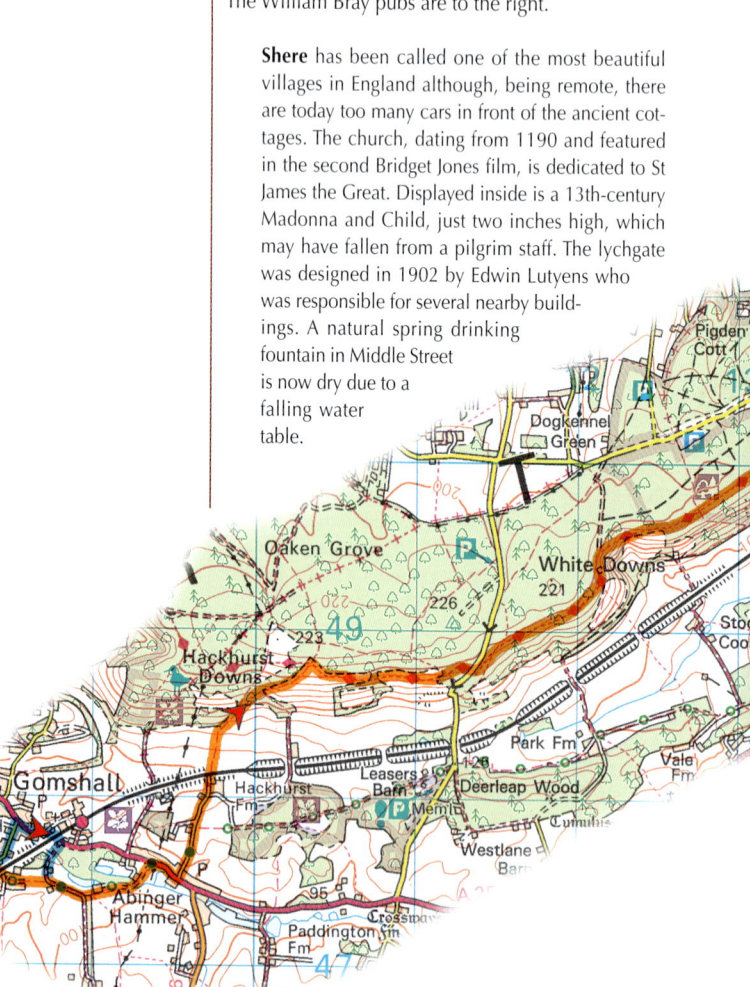

STAGE 5 – GUILDFORD TO BOX HILL

The White Horse was built in 1425. The William Bray recalls the antiquary and lord of the manor who in the 1760s identified sections of the PW.

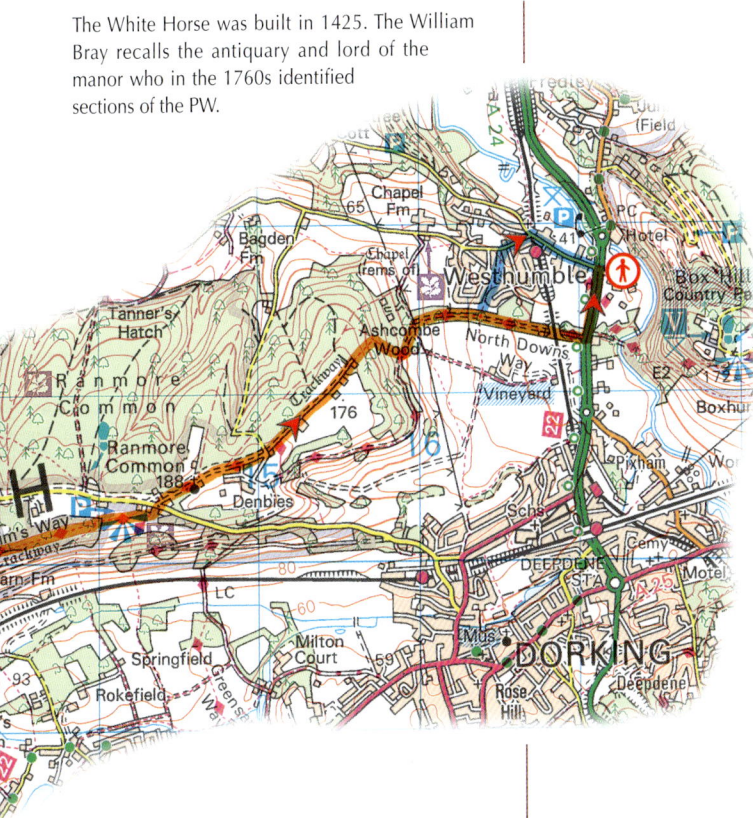

From The White Horse continue across The Square to the church and follow Church Lane. Just beyond Church Hill (right) take the enclosed footpath which runs quickly uphill. At a cross path go left along the side of a field which begins to go downhill. At the bottom the way becomes enclosed to climb gently uphill. On reaching new houses (left) and a T-junction bear left to follow Gravelpits Lane to a road by Monks House (right). Cross over and take the road ahead, High View, passing a post box and bus shelter (left). ▶

The house behind has an unusual hedge.

THE PILGRIMS' WAY

For Gomshall station
At the end of High View, follow Goose Green to Gomshall Mill Inn on the Tilling Bourne and turn right along the main road (½ mile/0.8km).

From Gomshall station
Walk down to the main road and cross with care. Turn left through the pedestrian tunnel under the railway and go right, down Wonham Way which crosses the Tilling Bourne. The PW joins from the right at a bend (¼ mile/0.4km).

At the far end of High View, where the road bends to become Goose Green, go right, through the railway arch. After a short distance go left into Towerhill Farm. After the farmhouse (right) bear half left on the narrow footpath.

Go right at Wonham Way which soon runs gently uphill. After the top of the hill bend go left by Southbrooks Farmhouse. However, after a few yards keep to the right of The Barn and where the path divides go left. The high path soon runs down to a hard surface road on Gomshall Marsh. Turn right here to follow the path round a bend, over the Tilling Bourne and past houses (left). The way meets the main road almost opposite Hunters Moon Farm.

Blatchford Down view

STAGE 5 – GUILDFORD TO BOX HILL

Turn right along the main road, which confusingly changes its name from Dorking Road to Guildford Road. Ahead is **Abinger Hammer** clock tower and village green. The Old Post Office tea room, the last refreshment before Westhumble, is just beyond the clock tower.

> **'Hammer'** comes from the 'trip hammer' installed in 1557 at an iron mill on the site of the watercress beds. The church, dedicated to St James the Great and with a large Norman nave, is on high ground more than a mile to the south-east. However, despite its distance from the track, it is claimed as a halting place for pilgrims on their way to Canterbury and Santiago de Compostela. The landmark clock in the main street, with a blacksmith figure hammering out the hours, dates from 1909.

At the clock turn left up Hackhurst Lane. After a climb the narrow lane runs down to a cottage (left). Bear left through **Hackhurst Farm** and over the level crossing on the North Downs Link railway line. The path narrows and then widens to become a wooded hollow with yew trees as it climbs the hillside. Keep forward at a junction (by a signpost) and ignore another turning. Where the way suddenly runs into the open go right through a kissing gate onto **Blatchford Down** where there are two seats.

From here the way coincides with the NDW. The path across the grass drops slightly before running along a ledge, past pill boxes (right and soon left), with a view into the valley (right). Go through a kissing gate by a gateway ahead and continue into woodland. Ignore turnings and soon the way bears to the left and then right to run steeply down a hollow to a road. Cross diagonally to find the path continuing by a concrete stone marked with an E. The way bears left gently uphill into woodland and past a pill box (left). ▶ The path again becomes wooded and passes close to another pill box (right). Also visible, with its squat early Norman tower, is **Wotton Church**.

> When the trees clear after a kissing gate there is a view (right) down to Dorking where the spire of St Martin's Church is often visible.

At a junction with a deep path joining from the right go through the gateway by a pill box (right). Beyond the gate walk up onto the bank ahead. After 130 yards (120 metres) look carefully for a signpost to turn right. There is also an acorn mark on a tree (right). The sometimes indistinct path, according to season, runs along a wooded shoulder above Pickett's Hole (right) where there are many beech trees. Occasionally the way is obvious and after curving slightly left is straight. After a second cross path there is another view before the path continues beyond a barrier. The way is now straight as it runs through woodland known as The Spains.

At the far end a kissing gate leads to Steer's Field viewpoint. Take the path slightly right ahead, and after passing back gardens (left) go left to find a kissing gate. Walk half right across grass to a road junction on **Ranmore Common**. The Old Post Office, an isolated house, is opposite. Go ahead down the road opposite. Soon there is Ranmore Church (right).

> George Gilbert Scott designed **Ranmore Church** in 1859 for George Cubitt who inherited the Denbies estate from his father Thomas, builder and developer of Pimlico. He had rebuilt the mansion in the style of Osborne House on the Isle of Wight which he also built having collaborated with Prince Albert in the design. George Cubitt's church here was intended for his family and 300 staff. Since 1991 the harvest festival has included grapes from the new vineyard. Denbies House was demolished in 1953.

Continue along the road passing a long hedge behind which Denbies House mansion once stood. Where the road turns sharp left keep forward past Denbies House lodge (right) to follow a concrete path.

> The Romans produced wine at **Denbies** and vines were again planted in 1986. Now it is England's largest vineyard with most of the award-winning

STAGE 5 – GUILDFORD TO BOX HILL

wines sold at the visitors' centre which has a cafe (open 9.30am–4pm) and offers overnight accommodation.

Soon the NDW turns right while the PW continues ahead. Stay on this path to pass Dairy Cottages and stables. At the end, where the concrete gives way to a rough track, still keep forward past Ashcombe Cottage (right).

The path runs steeply downhill through woodland. At the bottom go right where the ground continues to fall. At a T-junction there is a glimpse ahead of the vineyard with a path running down to the visitors' centre.

Turn left along the hard surface path. Where this swings right keep forward on a wide path running under trees. This bears round to the right and runs gently downhill by a wood to the left with more glimpses of the **vineyard** (right). Halfway down there is a gate on the right leading through the vineyard to the visitors' centre and cafe.

> A short cut to Box Hill & Westhumble station is to the left of the wide walk. Go through a kissing gate and across a field to another kissing gate. Follow a narrow passage which crosses a residential road. At the far end turn right along Chapel Lane. After white fencing there is a path above the road which crosses the railway bridge at the station (½ mile/0.8km).

Continue down the wide path, an ancient trackway, to a gateway. Keep forward on a now metalled way past a house (right) and under the railway bridge to reach gates at a main road. The ancient track continues over the dual carriageway. However, there is a foot tunnel for walkers to the left just beyond the turning to Box Hill & Westhumble station.

For Box Hill & Westhumble station
Turn left along the dual carriageway and go left into Westhumble Street and past The Stepping Stones pub (360 yards/0.3km).

STAGE 6
Box Hill to Merstham

Start	Westhumble Street at Box Hill
Finish	Quality Street at Merstham
Distance	9¾ miles (15.6km)
Time	3½hrs
Maps	OS Explorer 146; Landranger 187
Refreshments	Pubs at Westhumble and Betchworth; tea hut at Reigate Hill
Toilets	Burford Bridge car park at Westhumble
Public transport	Railway stations at Westhumble (Box Hill & Westhumble station), Betchworth and Merstham
Accommodation	Westhumble, Betchworth and Reigate Hill

After crossing the River Mole stepping stones, deep in woods, there is a steep climb up to a viewpoint path on the side of Box Hill. For most of this stage the path is on the side of the North Downs, but another steep climb comes at Reigate Hill where the reward is a view south across the town and north to The Shard at the London start. The climax is attractive Quality Street, with its theatrical and sweet associations, in Merstham.

From Box Hill & Westhumble station

Go right, down Westhumble Street to pass The Stepping Stones pub and reach the main road (360 yards/0.3km). Cross the dual carriageway by turning left for a short distance and walking through a pedestrian tunnel. Bear right on the far side.

Walk south along the road with the traffic to the right. At a second bus stop go left into a wide entrance. Keep forward past a car park and through trees by a high fence (right) to the River Mole. Cross on the stepping stones. (If the water is running high go downstream to a bridge.)

STAGE 6 – BOX HILL TO MERSTHAM

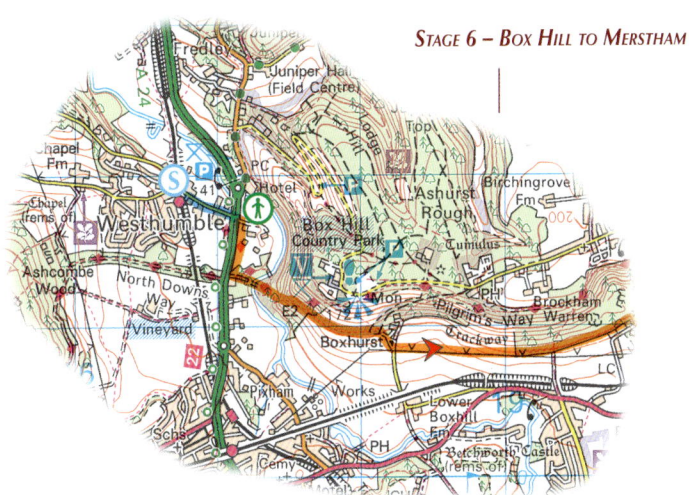

The **stones crossing**, on the line of a ford, was reopened in 1946 by Prime Minister Clement Attlee after wartime closure. His Home Secretary, James Chuter-Ede, from nearby Dorking paid for the new stones. The River Mole rises near Gatwick Airport and joins the Thames at Hampton Court.

map continues on page 80

Box Hill stepping stones

On the far side go up steps and ahead up a wide path. The alternative path from the bridge joins on the left. Soon the way becomes steep as it rises quickly up the side of Box Hill.

Box Hill takes its name from box trees that grew in great abundance until they were cut down in the early 19th century. Jane Austen saw them when she made it a setting for a picnic in *Emma*. Author George Meredith, who lived from 1868 to 1909 at remote Flint Cottage on the hill, said, 'Nowhere in England is richer foliage, or wilder downs and fresher woodlands'. At the top, where there are views of Dorking and Betchworth below and Chanctonbury Ring on the South Downs, there is a cafe.

At the start of the third flight of steps go right, on a narrow path into the trees. The way, which bears slightly

STAGE 6 – BOX HILL TO MERSTHAM

left, can in season be sometimes indistinct. Later it climbs a little and soon is near a field (right). ▶ On the way there is a kissing gate. After another gateway the path joins a track to curve right, downhill, to a lane at Boxhurst.

At once cross over to go through a kissing gate and past a redundant stile. The path, running ahead and with pylons to the right, is on the line of the PW as identified by early OS cartographers. Later the way begins to run gently uphill. Keep a drinking trough and the start of a field boundary to the right.

In the corner go through a kissing gate and ahead to a path junction. Turn right, downhill, where the path curves left to continue in an easterly direction just above fields (right). At kissing gates cross another path as it double bends downhill.

Here is the first of several good views of Dorking below.

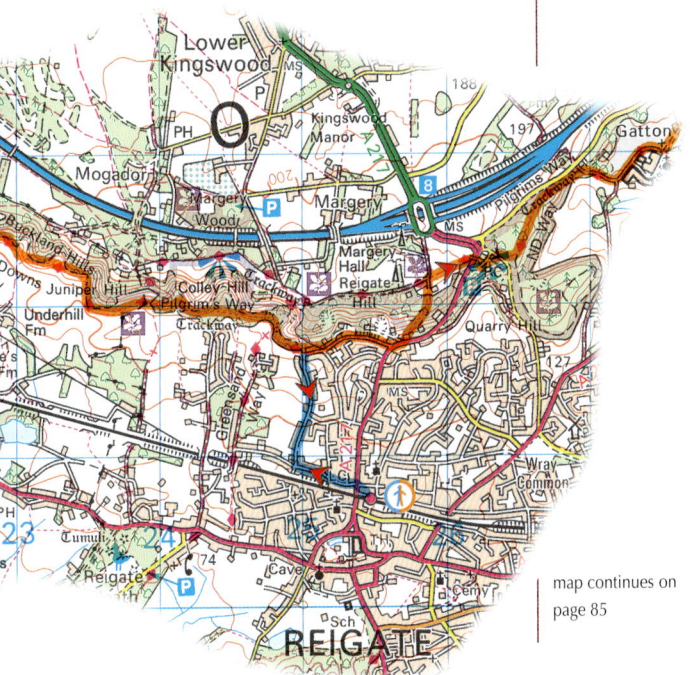

map continues on page 85

The Pilgrims' Way

Dorking from Box Hill path

A disused quarry to the left is hidden by trees but soon the path runs down to old lime kilns. The way continues to the right of the brickwork to again become a woodland path. Ignore cross paths and keep forward where the main track appears to bear up to the left. There is a handrail and steps where the path suddenly runs downhill and then uphill. The path climbs a little higher before suddenly stopping at more steps. Go left, with a handrail, up the steps to a track. Turn right and at once there is a view of a huge lime kiln tower (right).

The way, now briefly joined by the NDW, begins to run downhill. Keep left at a divide to reach a kissing gate. Follow the stony track ahead past cottages (left). Bear right at the end to the main road. Turn right past Betchworth Lodge and follow a raised path alongside the main road. At the end cross the level crossing to **Betchworth station**.

The station in **Betchworth**, opened in 1849, lies north of the village with the church, green and 17th-century Dolphin pub a mile away.

STAGE 6 – BOX HILL TO MERSTHAM

St Michael's church, which featured in the 1994 film *Four Weddings and A Funeral*, is mainly 13th century but has a trace of Saxon work in the tower. From 1199 to 1539 its patron was Southwark Priory (now Cathedral). The arrival of the railway encouraged lime mining here, which only ended in 1936, with a branch line running to the pits.

The PW continues on the far (south) side of the level crossing. At once go left by the gatepost to find the entrance to a footpath. The way rises to run alongside the railway embankment and later drops down to a kissing gate. On entering a field keep close to the railway to reach a second kissing gate. Turn left along a lane to go under the line and bear right. Soon the way is alongside a field. On meeting another lane, by a level crossing, go left. The way runs past cottages and through **Kemp's Farm** to reach a gateway.

Bear half left across a field aiming for the left end of a hedge. Here the NDW rejoins from a kissing gate. The way is ahead through a set back gateway and along a narrow enclosed path which soon begins to climb at the edge of Dawcombe Wood. Turn right at a junction where there are barriers. The path is still in woodland and ends by running steeply up a bank to a rutted track known as Buckland Lane.

Go right on the curving path passing under yew trees. After a short distance go up steps on the left. At the top the path runs ahead to turn east and run along the bottom of the **Buckland Hills**. ▶ Just after a path joins from the left there is a fork. Take the left branch which runs uphill through young trees. Round the corner there is a cross path and steps (left). But keep ahead.

The path continues to wind slightly until at the bottom of **Juniper Hill** it bends right to pass a National Trust sign. Then it bends left to run along a wooded shelf with glimpses of the grassy slope (left). At a junction the NDW turns sharp left uphill as the PW stays ahead through a tunnel of yews with fields seen to the right. The way suddenly veers half left to go up and down a bank.

There are occasional views into the valley (right) and sometimes the trees fall away to allow the path to run in the open.

The Pilgrims' Way

Path along the edge of Buckland Hills

Ignore a sharp turning (right) just before the way bears right to curve round the bottom of **Colley Hill's** grass Saddle Knob (left). Sometimes the path is close to the grass. Later, in trees, the path reaches a long flight of steps leading down to a disused pit. At the bottom the way double bends to continue east.

Go over a junction where an information board records the location of an old hearthstone mine. Soon the way bends south and, joined by the Greensand Way, east again. On meeting a metalled residential road on the edge of Reigate there is another National Trust Pilgrims' Way sign.

For Reigate station

On reaching Reigate at the NT sign turn right, downhill, go left at a crossroads into Somers Road and right at the main street for the station (¾ mile/1.2km).

The PW continues ahead up a slightly rising metalled road. Where it bends right go ahead up the narrow track which at once crosses a drive entrance. The walled PW runs ahead below **Reigate Hill** (left) for almost half a

STAGE 6 – BOX HILL TO MERSTHAM

mile, passing the Scouts' Jordan Heights entrance. At a cluster of cottages turn left up the Reigate Hill main road for just a few yards. Go left and at once right by a large Craig Cottage sign.

A path straight ahead, which is soon a rising wooded hollow, climbs the hill to pass lonely Rock Farm (right). At a junction go right to rejoin the NDW. The Shard in central London (left) can be seen on a clear day as the path drops gently to cross Reigate Hill footbridge, flanked by mounting blocks, and reaches a tea hut at the Reigate Hill viewpoint.

REIGATE HILL

The supporters on Reigate's coat of arms are two 12th-century pilgrims both holding a staff and wearing a shell in their hat. Augustinian Reigate Priory, opposite the castle, was founded in about 1210 and closed in 1536. The order's Southwark Priory was the parish church's patron. St Thomas of Canterbury Chapel stood on the Old Town Hall site in the middle of the High Street. The Red Cross Inn was a pilgrim hospital for those venturing down into the town. The first footbridge carrying the PW over the deeply cut road on the hill was a suspension bridge opened in 1828. The present crossing, the earliest example of a concrete footbridge, was erected in 1910.

Walk across the National Trust car park to its entrance. With care, cross Wray Lane to take the path into the **Gatton woodland** opposite. The way bears right. At once go left, leaving the NDW. The wide path is marked on the post as 'Millennium Trail' and runs downhill to a yew tree where the NDW rejoins from the right. Keep forward to a road by the stone Tower Lodge (left).

Soon there is a seat and a view across Gatton parkland (right).

Go right along the metalled road. ◄ Pass through a gateway into the Gatton Park grounds. A Millennium Stones feature is to the right.

GATTON PARK

The name is derived from a gate on the PW although the exact line of the original path is uncertain here. The OS suggests it might have run past the modern buildings and the thatched lodge. The estate received borough status from Henry VI who wanted members of Parliament to support his marriage to Margaret of Anjou. The 'town' continued to elect two members until the 1832 Great Reform Act. The mansion, once home of Sir Jeremiah Colman of Colman's mustard fame, was gutted by fire in 1934. The thatched North Lodge dates from about 1830. St Andrew's Church, on a Norman site and open first Sunday in the month, is mainly Tudor with an interior resembling a college chapel. Gatton Park is now occupied by the Royal Alexandra & Albert School.

Stay on the park road as it bears round to the left passing some buildings. By the modern school chapel (left) there is a junction. Go half right only to visit St Andrew's Church. The PW continues left along the park road to reach the thatched North Lodge. Keep forward on the road. Soon after it bends right, go left between a beech hedge and a white picket fence. Just before the Dower House turn right. The way leaves buildings behind to run ahead and eventually reach a kissing gate. Keep forward and soon cross a concrete golf club road. Here, before a nearby motorway was built, the PW used to run ahead direct to Merstham church but now the path bears right and across open ground. Drop down through trees and cross a stream feeding the nearby lake. Keep forward over a cricket ground and up a concrete path to pass the old Home Farm barn (right) and reach Quality Street.

For Merstham station
Go left along Quality Street and right down Old Mill Lane to the main road. Station Road is ahead (350 yards/0.3km).

STAGE 7
Merstham to Oxted

Start	Quality Street, Merstham
Finish	Chalkpit Lane, Oxted
Distance	8 miles (12.8km)
Time	3hrs
Maps	OS Explorer 146; Landranger 187
Refreshments	Pubs at Merstham, Whitehill and Oxted
Public transport	Railway stations at Merstham and Oxted

The original route from Merstham to the top of the North Downs has been changed by the arrival of two motorways and two railway lines. However, the view is fascinating, and nearby Chaldon Church has a disturbing wall painting which gave pilgrims much to meditate on as they continued their walk. Before Oxted there is another arresting view as the path goes down steps above a railway tunnel.

From Merstham station
Turn right out of the station to walk along Station Road. Cross the main road by The Railway Arms to Old Mill Lane. Turn right into Quality Street (350 yards/0.3km).

> The attractive **Quality Street**, once the main road to Brighton, is named after JM Barrie's play *Quality Street* which opened at London's Vaudeville Theatre in 1902 and ran for over a year. Seymour Hicks and Ellaline Terriss, the actors who played the two main characters, Captain Brown and Phoebe Throssel, lived in the 15th-century Old Forge at the street's north end. The famous tin of sweets, launched in 1936 by Mackintosh's of Halifax to coincide with the release of the *Quality Street* film, had a bow-fronted shop on the lid similar to houses here which include 17th- and 18th-century buildings. A fair

The Pilgrims' Way

is held in the street every summer under a charter granted by Edward III.

Walk down Quality Street. Just beyond the Old Forge (right), and before the gateway ahead, bear right, down a pathway which crosses high above a nearly always noisy M25 motorway and leads to a lane below Merstham church. Cross Gatton Bottom lane and go up the steps to a kissing gate leading to the churchyard.

The manor belonged to Canterbury Cathedral from at least Norman times until Henry VIII's reign and the patron of **Merstham church** remains the Archbishop of Canterbury. Most of the church dates from the early 13th century but the font is from the period when Becket was archbishop. A wall painting which lasted until around 1865 is known to have depicted a bishop and four knights with drawn

map continues on page 92

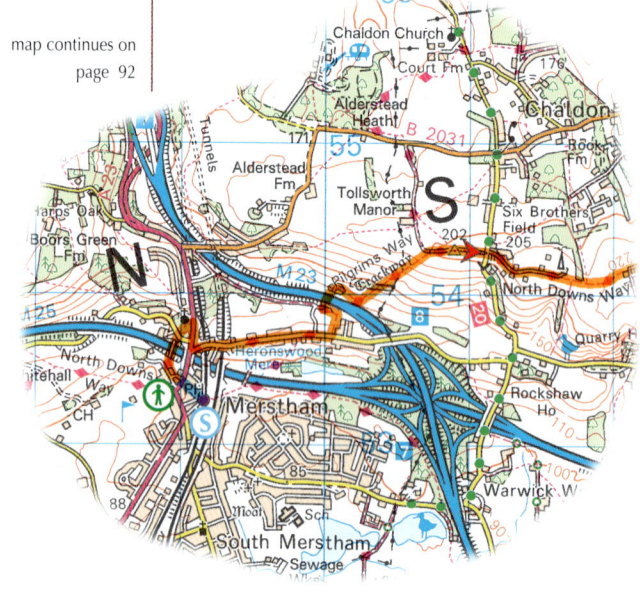

The Old Forge in Quality Street

swords. It is open 9.30am to 4.30pm (3.30pm in winter). A roadside well to the west, where the dovecot comes into view, is said to have been used by pilgrims.

Continue past the church (left) to reach the lychgate. Turn right for a few yards along the main road before using the traffic island to cross over. Continue along the road to pass a bus stop and go left into Rockshaw Road. There is a pavement on the right. The road crosses high over two railway lines. After Bramley House (left) there is a long gap before the next house, Sarum (left), opposite Noddyshall Cottage (right). Turn left down the side of Sarum on a narrow path running gently downhill through trees and undergrowth. At the bottom the path bears left for a short distance. At a junction go under the M23 motorway.

On the north side the path bears round to the right to start a climb up the hill. Pass an apple tree and continue uphill. ▶ The path enters another field at a corner.

In early summer the way is through cow parsley.

THE PILGRIMS' WAY

Drunk pilgrim with empty bottle in Chaldon church wall painting

At the top pass through a belt of trees. Continue half right up to the very top of the hill. Here there is a spectacular view south. Bear right onto an enclosed path known as Pilgrims' Lane. There are views (right) and a trig point. Ahead is Hilltop Lane on the edge of **Chaldon**. To visit Chaldon Church only, just under a mile away, turn left along the road.

The west end of **Chaldon Church**, dating from 1086, is covered with a Ladder of Salvation wall painting featuring a drunken naked pilgrim holding an empty wine bottle. It was painted in about 1200, thirty years after the murder of Becket, when the church was in the care of Merton Abbey where the saint had been a pupil. On a pillar near the door there is a pilgrim mark in the shape of a T for Thomas. The church is open 10am to 4pm (winter 10am–3pm), and there is tea and cake on Sundays (April–October) 3pm–4.30pm.

The PW crosses Hilltop Lane where the track is signed both Hilltop Farm and PW. Pilgrims' Lane continues ahead passing several isolated houses. After Hilltop (left with a clock and a view) the way is alongside woodland and fields (right). The rough lane later goes down and uphill before passing Willey Park Farm, with an old flint building (right) which dates from 1665.

▶ Take the right fork. After passing a wood (left) the way meets a road at the top of **White Hill**. Opposite is a tall tower. Visible to the left is The Harrow pub on the very edge of scattered Chaldon.

> As the track divides there is a view north (left) where The Shard and other central London buildings are often visible.

The Harrow, once two cottages built in the 16th century, was the Home Guard headquarters during World War II, when the ridge was thought to need defending during an invasion. A map remains on the wall. This is the highest pub on the PW. The nearby Whitehill Tower, looking like an abandoned church, is a folly built in 1862 by a farmer in memory of his son.

For Caterham station
At White Hill go left past The Harrow and downhill along Stanstead Road which leads directly to the station (1½ miles/2.4km).

The PW continues down War Coppice Road passing the folly (left). After The Mound entrance (right) the road is downhill. At the crossroads go onto the path ahead by Hextalls Lane entrance. The way is now parallel to the road (left). Keep on the path through the wood. Where it joins a higher path still keep forward. Ignore an immediate right-hand path. The way runs downhill to be joined by a path from the right before rising. Many of the trees are yew. At a fork take the right-hand minor path to walk

THE PILGRIMS' WAY

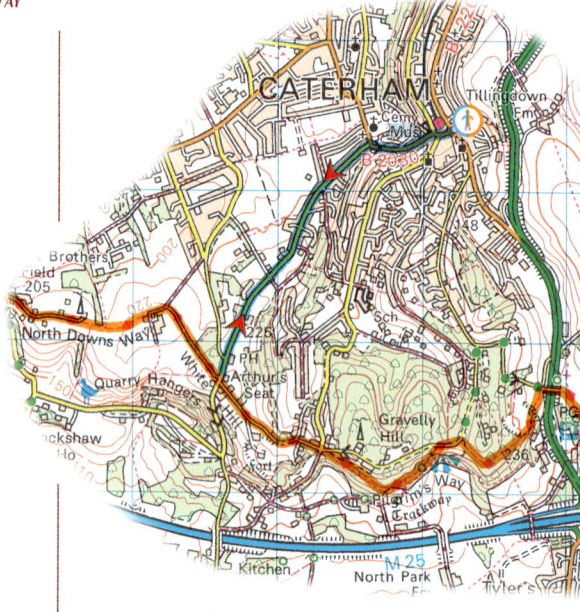

out onto a wide
area of grass at **Gravelly Hill**
known as the Caterham viewpoint.

Walk to the far end of the grass with the road on the left and turn right, onto a track at a gate. Keep ahead past the second seat as the path drops down to turn sharp left into woodland. There are again several yews. ◀ After a cross path the main track goes downhill. At a divide go right. Almost at once the path is above a wooded drop (right) before arriving at steps. Go down two flights of steps. At the bottom follow the path as it turns north. On reaching a road at a bend do not go ahead but right, across the wide footbridge over the A22.

Keep forward to a gap in a hedge and turn right along a track. After a short distance, just after an electricity sub station (left), leave the track by going half left by an NDW signpost. The woodland path soon bears round to the left to go down steps to a road at The Devils Hole. To the left is a large warehouse. Go ahead along a path at the side

Unseen behind the trees to the left is Pilgrim Fort earthwork.

STAGE 7 – MERSTHAM TO OXTED

of Quarry Cottage's garage. Climb up steps and turn right along a partly concrete surface lane. Pass Winders Hill Cottages (right) and continue

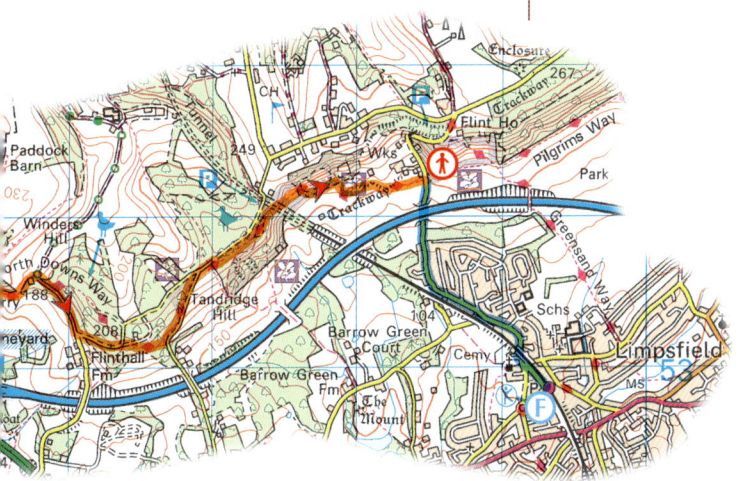

beyond a yellow gate. The way runs uphill. Soon there is a small vineyard (right). Ignore any turnings to reach South Lodge (right) by the entrance to Woldingham School (left).

Woldingham School in Marden Park, once occupied by William Wilberforce, has been a girls school since 1946. In the late 12th century it was part of the manor held by Richard de Lucy who founded Lesnes Abbey (see Stage 2a).

Here the NDW goes ahead while the PW continues (right) where the ancient route is now on a hard surface. On meeting a road do not go ahead but turn sharp left to climb the hill. ▶ At Hanging Wood Forest Farm entrance go right, to an enclosed path. The NDW rejoins here. The way curves downhill to a kissing gate. Go through the gate. The path quickly climbs above the road (right) on

Take care on the hairpin bend at the beginning.

THE PILGRIMS' WAY

Here there is also a handy seat and information board.

the edge of Hanging Wood. At the top of **Tandridge Hill** the path at last joins the road. Go ahead to the junction.

Turn right. After a short distance go right, to the start of two footpaths. Take the one which at first is alongside the road (left). The way, in Grangers Hill woods, comes to a T-junction. Go right, downhill, and where the path turns left there is a view east and across Oxted. ◄

Continue ahead, past another seat, to reach a junction of steps. Bear right to take the long flight descending into the valley. Ahead is a view directly down the railway line running into Oxted. Trains run under the steps. The original line of the Pilgrims' Way can be seen passing across the end of the 1878 railway tunnel entrance. Halfway down there is another handy seat and viewpoint.

At the bottom the path bears left along the edge of the wood on the side of Oxted Downs. Pass a stile (right) and at the end go through the kissing gate. The path now goes downhill to a hidden kissing gate. Still continue ahead by a field boundary (left) to a corner where the original Pilgrims' Way joins from the right. Turn left to briefly join the line of the ancient track. The path stays near the boundary with a hidden quarry (left) and leads directly to a kissing gate and a short enclosed path. At Chalkpit Lane, on the edge of Oxted, turn right.

The PW continues up steps on the left after a few yards.

For Oxted station

Keep ahead on Chalkpit Lane to go under the M25. Soon after the first houses there is a pavement on the left. Bear left into Gordons Way which becomes Barrow Green Road. Pass under the railway. Here the church is to the right and Station Approach to the left (1 mile/1.6km).

Original line of the Pilgrims' Way outside Oxted

STAGE 8
Oxted to Otford

Start	Chalkpit Lane, Oxted
Finish	Otford
Distance	12 miles (19.3km)
Time	5hrs
Maps	OS Explorer 146 and 147; Landranger 187 and 188
Refreshments	Pubs at Dunton Green and Otford
Toilets	Chevening churchyard
Public transport	Railway stations at Oxted and Otford; bus 246 at Westerham Hill
Accommodation	Oxted and Dunton Green

Here the Pilgrims' Way passes from Surrey into Kent. It also crosses two estates where, although the families who lived there are gone and the properties now owned by trustees, walkers continue to be diverted off the ancient line because it runs close to the mansions. Stately Titsey and Chevening are linked by one of the longest stretches of the PW to have been given a hard surface, although fortunately the way has not become a main road. There are no pubs until almost the end. But the Chevening diversion affords one of the best views of the house and its beautiful setting familiar to Jane Austen.

From Oxted station

Leave the station by the western side and go right, along Station Approach. At the junction go left and right to walk under the railway bridge. Follow the road ahead, ignoring all turnings. A short distance after passing under the M25 bridge, look for the NDW waymark by steps on the right (1 mile/1.6km).

The path turns left to run up to a kissing gate. At once bear left up a very steep slope to a seat. Pass the seat (left) to follow a path alongside a fence (right). The way veers

The Pilgrims' Way

OXTED

The Crown and The Old Bell in the old High Street date from Tudor times. The church, on a low mound to the north-east of the old village centre, has a 12th-century tower and a 14th-century chancel arch. The approach from 'Old Oxted' in the west towards the railway station is up a Surrey Tudor-style shopping street created in the 1930s. To the east, Oxted merges with Limpsfield where the farmhouse architecture owes more to nearby Kent than Surrey. Composer Frederick Delius and conductor Sir Thomas Beecham are buried in ita churchyard.

Oxted church

On the way the path crosses the Greenwich Meridian line which is marked by a plaque (left).

slightly away before returning to the fence at a kissing gate in the corner. A short passage leads to a field below the Titsey Plantation (left). The spire of Titsey church can be seen ahead. ◄ After several kissing gates, the path goes down steps to a chalky hollow. Turn left to walk uphill. Ignore all tempting turnings.

Titsey Park is to the right as the way climbs steeply through the trees to the top of Botley Hill, the highest point on the Pilgrims' Way. At the road junction turn right, past a car park, and where the pavement ends cross the road to find a footpath opposite. The woodland path

STAGE 8 – OXTED TO OTFORD

later rises to stay close to the road (right). Pass steps where the NDW leaves the path. The PW continues ahead. Soon there is a fence (left) as the way turns south down the hill through trees to the junction of White Lane with Titsey Hill. Now join the road (right) to continue downhill with care. Walk on the right and shortly there is a wide verge. Titsey Park and the mansion are to the right and the church is on the left.

At Titsey church turn left into Pilgrims' Lane to pass Church Cottage and Forge Cottage (right). The road runs gently up and down, passing remote houses and farms, for five miles. But first there are Evelyn Avenue houses and **Pilgrims Farm** (left). Pass Rectory Lane (left) and, almost immediately at a bend, Clacket Lane which gives its name to a famous service station a mile to the south.

At a staggered crossroads with a post box and Kent Cottages continue ahead over Croydon Road to enter Kent. Half a mile on, past a vineyard

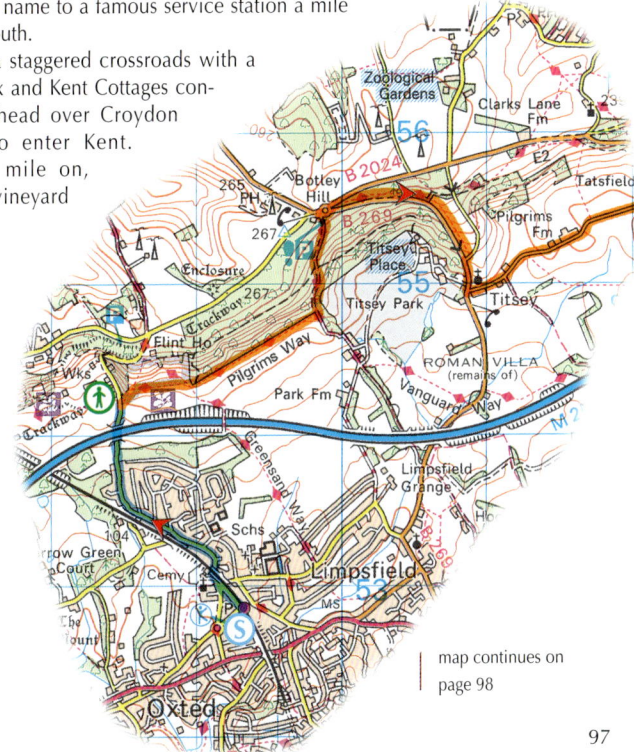

map continues on page 98

The Pilgrims' Way

TITSEY

The mansion, successor to a Roman villa, dates largely from 1775 but incorporates some of the Tudor house purchased in 1534 by Sir John Gresham who later became Lord Mayor of London. It remained with his descendants until the late 20th century when the Titsey Trust was formed. The house and grounds are open on some summer days (www.titsey.org). The original church, dating from at least the 13th century and dedicated to St James the Great, was 400 yards to the west in Titsey Park. The T-junction was a crossroads until the ancient pilgrim route was closed. A new church was built on the present site in 1776 and rebuilt in 1860–61 to a design by JL Pearson. After being declared redundant in 1973 it passed to the Titsey Trust. Church Cottage and the forge opposite date from 1673.

There are more wide views as the road winds ahead.

(right), is **Betsoms Farm** at a crossroads with bus stops on Westerham Hill. After another half mile pass the long entrance to Pilgrim House (left) and Force Green Lane (right). ◀ Go over the **Hogtrough Hill** crossroads by lonely Hogtrough Cottage (left). **Court Lodge Farm** can be seen down the hill (right). The rolling road is a long hedged way as far as the Brasted Hill Road junction. Here go right and left to find the PW continuing east.

Pass a tree-lined farm entrance (left) to finally reach a T-junction at the bottom of Sundridge Hill. Turn left to almost at once pass the continuation of the ancient track (right) as it enters **Chevening Park**. This is closed to walkers who must continue uphill.

The steep lane leads to Knockholt, but before the village go right at Keepers Cottage through a wide gateway to enter Chevening Park.

STAGE 8 – OXTED TO OTFORD

Keep forward down a long woodland path which in season is alive with game birds. Ignore any minor turnings but where the main track divides go half right. The path runs downhill to a viewpoint with a seat. Here is the first view of Chevening House.

Chevening House was designed by Inigo Jones in the 1630s and enlarged with side wings when bought in 1717 by Chancellor of the Exchequer Lord Stanhope. In 1792 his grandson closed his section of the Pilgrims' Way to stop travellers passing the house. The grounds include a maze planted in 1822, a lake and a double hexagonal walled kitchen garden. Prime Minister Lord Rosebery described Chevening as 'paradise' and Kipling thought it 'enchanted'. The 7th earl was the last Lord Stanhope,

map continues on page 102

The Pilgrims' Way

a cabinet minister and founder of the National Maritime Museum, who died in 1967 leaving the house to the nation. It is now the official residence of the foreign secretary and other senior ministers.

The path bears left downhill to a stile to run outside the wood (left) down the side of a field. Ahead is a short steep and wide wooded path running down to a squeeze stile where there is another view of the house. Continue downhill by the trees (left) on the edge of the pasture which rolls down towards the Pilgrims' Way and the house. The walled garden can be seen below.

Go through a kissing gate and bear round to the left. At a gate go right, by a stile, and along a fence (left). At the driveway cross the stile on the far side to continue on the other side of the fence. Bear left at the field corner to find a stile round the corner. Cross an estate road to go over another stile. This may be disorienting but the way is ahead to the wood. Cross a stile and go right. (Only go left to walk up to Knockholt village.) The tree-lined path soon crosses the barely visible ancient Pilgrims' Way line. There is a glimpse of the house to the right.

Approaching the PW's highest point

At the end cross another estate road to enter Chevening churchyard.

Chevening House

CHEVENING CHURCH

The dedication of this PW church is to St Botolph, patron saint of travellers. It was built by 1262 and the tower added in about 1518. On the south wall of the sanctuary is a memorial to Robert Cranmer, a relative of Archbishop Thomas Cranmer and owner of Saltwood Castle near Dover where Becket's assassins stayed the night before the murder. There are also elaborate Stanhope family memorials. Jane Austen's uncle, John, was rector from 1813 to 1851. His parsonage (north side of the church and demolished 1941) was a model for Mr Collins' vicarage in *Pride and Prejudice*. The church's patron has long been the Archbishop of Canterbury giving rise to the beautiful parish being known as 'the Archbishop's Garden'. Geoffrey Howe was a regular worshipper when foreign secretary from 1983 to 1989.

The PW leaves the churchyard by a gate near the cross in the south-east corner. Go ahead down a grass way which soon narrows. At a redundant, and usually overgrown, kissing gate keep ahead along the side (left) of a field. On the far side the way becomes enclosed. Where the way

THE PILGRIMS' WAY

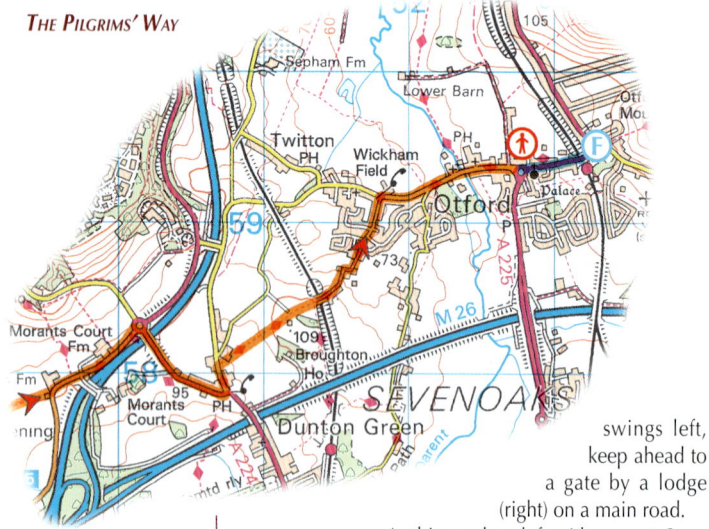

swings left, keep ahead to a gate by a lodge (right) on a main road.

At this road go left with care. ◄ Soon the North Downs Way joins from the left and a little later there is a pavement on the right. Follow this pavement round a corner and over the M25. On the far side the pavement switches sides.

Stay on this road to reach the Rose & Crown at Dunton Green. Go left up London Road. At the side of Donnington Manor Hotel (right) go right. A straight path runs ahead and up the side of two fields. After trees at the top of the hill go over a sloping field to a gate and stile at a railway bridge. A metalled lane runs downhill passing lavender fields, and after a double bend continues through a residential area to meet the main road, Pilgrims Way West. Go right along the road to cross the **River Darent** and reach Otford's High Street and pond.

For Otford station
From the pond at the end of the High Street walk along Station Road and bear right before the railway bridge (¼ mile/0.4km).

Walkers may wish to stay on the left-hand side at the bend for safety.

STAGE 9
Otford to Wrotham

Start	Otford
Finish	Wrotham recycling centre
Distance	5¾ miles (9.2km)
Time	2½hrs
Maps	OS Explorer 147; Landranger 188
Refreshments	Tea shops at Otford; pubs at Otford and Kemsing
Public transport	Railway stations at Otford and Wrotham (Borough Green & Wrotham station); bus to railway station at Wrotham
Accommodation	Wrotham

Otford is where the London route joins the path from Winchester, and where in 1851 one antiquary claimed that this was the true start of the pilgrim road. The converged ways continue east to the hidden village of Kemsing which has its own saint, Edith. Wrotham has an unusually large church. Be aware that although Wrotham has a railway station it is downhill away from the village and best reached by bus.

From Otford station
Either from the main station house or the London 'down' platform walk to Station Road. Turn left for the village centre (¼ mile/0.4km) at the pond roundabout.

The route from London joins the High Street opposite Otford Tearooms.

Go down the the right, or south, side of the church and follow the path ahead below a long brick wall (left) to leave the churchyard at a gate. After a double bend there is a view (right) across Church Field where St Thomas Becket's well is located on the far side.

Go ahead only for Otford Station. The route continues sharp right on a still enclosed path. At the next junction go left over stiles at the railway line. (Before crossing

The Pilgrims' Way

OTFORD

Otford is famous for its unique duck pond roundabout complete with a duck house. Becket was associated with the village while still chancellor, for as a deacon he had been nominally assigned the church benefice. The manor belonged to the archbishop and when Becket attained that office he stayed here during his first year, 1162. He is said to have struck the ground with his crosier to obtain water. There is a Becket's Well in a garden and spring water runs in front of Otford Palace. The ruined palace seen now is half the north front of a rebuild for Archbishop William Warham who crowned Henry VIII and Katharine of Aragon. The king made the new palace his first overnight stop from Greenwich on his way to the Field of the Cloth of Gold summit in France in May 1520. The Bull inn has a fireplace, panelling and a settle which may have come from the palace. Opposite is the church hall built in 1909 to a design by Edwin Lutyens when his brother William was vicar.

Otford pond and church

A surviving fragment of Otford Palace

look and listen.) On the far side a passage leads to a road. Cross over to find the way continuing.

The metalled way is enclosed before runnning along the edge of Oxenhill Woods (right). Ignore all turnings and stay on the path which joins Dynes Road. Still keep forward to reach, after almost a mile (1.49km), St Edith's Well at the junction of the High Street and St Edith's Road (right) by The Bell.

Take the footpath north of the well to climb up to the church. Turn left out of the church lychgate and through

STAGE 9 – OTFORD TO WROTHAM

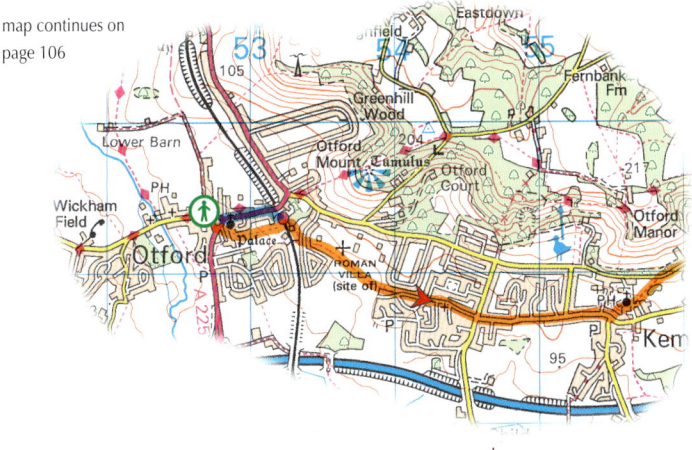

map continues on page 106

KEMSING

A legend claims that the knights who murdered Becket rode through here on their way to Canterbury and today the church is said to be haunted by a knight who appears on 29 December. The knights are unlikely to have come this way but the village was visited by passing pilgrims whose staves may have made the many indentations in the 13th-century church door. The holy well outside the deli-café recalls St Edith of Wilton who was born here in 961. The site was a convent founded simultaneously with one in Winchester by King Edgar as a penance for abducting Edith's mother Wulfrith from Wilton. Edith, whose statue can be seen outside the magnificent 1911 St Edith's Hall, was the sister of Ethelred the Unready. Kemsing had an arm bone relic of Edith to show pilgrims. On St Edith's Day, 16 September, there is well dressing and a procession.

Kemsing church porch door

a gateway. Pass a playground (left) and walk ahead over the grass with trees on both sides. Later pass tennis courts (right) and in the far corner of the grassland there is a short woodland path leading to steps. Go left to the road and turn right.

The PW continues ahead past the Kemsing path. After a crossroads and a junction there is a view of **St Clere** house and its grounds.

> **St Clere** was the home of the de St Clere family before the Wars of the Roses and was later owned by Anne Boleyn's family. The present house, incorporating some Tudor work, was built around 1630. Jane Austen knew William Evelyn, a relative of diarist John who lived here, although it is not known if she visited him. In 1878 it was purchased by Sir Mark Collet who became Governor of the Bank of England. Later his relative Montagu Norman lived here when also Governor. Ownership has descended within the family with the garden occasionally open to the public.

The path is mainly in a long tunnel of trees with an occasional view over countryside to the south.

When the tarmac road turns sharp right, keep ahead up the rising hedged way. Soon the track runs past White Hill wood (left) before crossing (at a slight angle) a road. ◄

On reaching Wrotham keep ahead. At a junction with Old London Road keep forward between Butts Hill Cottage (left) and Pilgrims Cottage (right). Soon the recreation ground appears (right). As the road bends right the church tower is seen ahead. The PW continues by the turning point (left).

STAGE 9 – OTFORD TO WROTHAM

For Borough Green & Wrotham station
Walk west along the High Street and continue following the road downhill (1 mile/1.6km). There is a bus service Monday to Saturday.

STAGE 10
Wrotham to Halling

Start	Wrotham recycling centre
Finish	Lower Halling
Distance	7¼ miles (11.6km)
Time	3½hrs
Maps	OS Explorer 147 and 148; Landranger 188 and 178
Refreshments	Pub at Wrotham
Toilets	Wrotham
Public transport	Railway stations at Wrotham (Borough Green & Wrotham) and Halling
Accommodation	Wrotham

This is the last stage before the Medway crossing is reached. Early on, signs indicate Wrotham Water which is not a lake but an area at the foot of the North Downs containing calcareous grassland including endangered orchids and butterflies. It is the only known site for the milkwort-feeding micromoth. After Trottiscliffe there are views down to industrial buildings in the Medway valley. The way rises steeply before dropping down into Halling on the river.

From Borough Green & Wrotham station
Go left from the station approach, and after crossing the motorway go left (1 mile/1.6km). There is a bus service Monday to Friday.

Start at the turning point in Pilgrims Way north of the church and next to the recreation ground. A short tarmac path runs uphill to a road. Go left over the M20 to a roundabout. Take the east exit marked Pilgrims Way. After a short distance a house called Former Rectory is on the same side as the pavement. The pavement soon runs out but look out for a path set back on the right running parallel with the lane. It starts opposite new houses.

STAGE 10 – WROTHAM TO HALLING

WROTHAM

The church, being on a 10th-century site, can claim to be the oldest in England dedicated to St George. The unusual passage below the tower is thought to have been created to allow outdoor processions to go round the church. Inside, the exceptionally wide nave leads to a 14th-century rood screen. Rector Richard Bancroft became Archbishop of Canterbury in 1604. George Moore, installed in 1800, was a relative of Jane Austen who visited while writing *Pride and Prejudice*. There has been an inn where The Bull stands since 1280 when the Old Palace next door was still used by archbishops travelling to and from Canterbury. Becket stayed for a night there on his final return from London less than a fortnight before his murder.

Tower archway at Wrotham church

Where the path ends at a stile opposite Cherry Trees, continue along the road which soon affords a view (right) and runs downhill passing an NT Wrotham Water sign.

Just after Field House (left) go through a kissing gate (left) to continue ahead above the lane. Later pass through two kissing gates flanking a gate before walking up and down to another kissing gate above steps. Turn left along the lane. Pass a house and weatherboarded cottage. Just after a footpath entrance (left) go through a kissing gate (left) to again walk just inside a field and alongside the road. The way climbs to a kissing gate leading to woodland.

When the path returns to the lane, now traffic free, turn left and at a fork go right while the NDW takes the other branch. The way is at first between high hedges. Later it runs on the edge of woodland and at a curve there is the view of a house. Beyond another NT sign the path

THE PILGRIMS' WAY

passes a brick wall below a thatched house on Vigo Hill. At the road go right to pass Pilgrim House (left). As the road bends, keep forward with the PW.

As the PW passes below the wooded hill (left), part of **Trosley Country Park**, it has a hard surface. Soon there can be a glimpse of Trottiscliffe Church

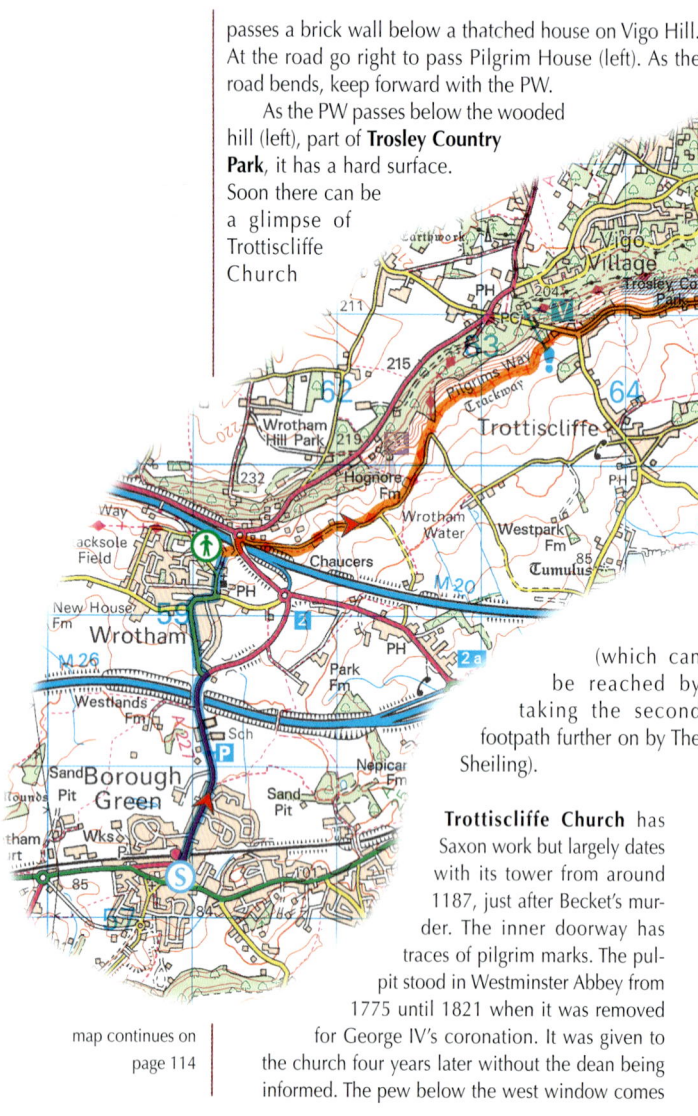

(which can be reached by taking the second footpath further on by The Sheiling).

Trottiscliffe Church has Saxon work but largely dates with its tower from around 1187, just after Becket's murder. The inner doorway has traces of pilgrim marks. The pulpit stood in Westminster Abbey from 1775 until 1821 when it was removed for George IV's coronation. It was given to the church four years later without the dean being informed. The pew below the west window comes

map continues on page 114

STAGE 10 – WROTHAM TO HALLING

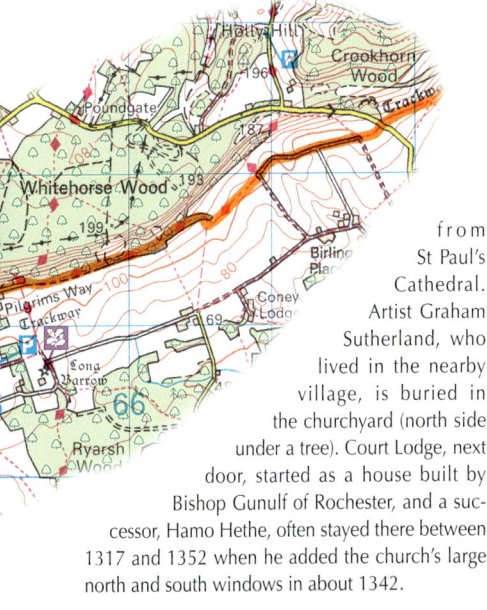

from St Paul's Cathedral. Artist Graham Sutherland, who lived in the nearby village, is buried in the churchyard (north side under a tree). Court Lodge, next door, started as a house built by Bishop Gunulf of Rochester, and a successor, Hamo Hethe, often stayed there between 1317 and 1352 when he added the church's large north and south windows in about 1342.

Whitehorse Wood

THE PILGRIMS' WAY

> Alternative return route from Trottiscliffe church: From the church return to the PW by going left, out of the gate, passing between cottages, going left up a steep path to a squeeze stile and ahead across a field. Turn left along Pinesfield Lane and right at the end.

At a junction by Harpwood, where the NDW joins, keep forward. After a few yards pass steps (left) as the way becomes a tunnel of trees below **Whitehorse Wood** on the hill (left). After about ¾ mile (1.2km) a wide track joins from the left. Here there is a lonely brick storage building. The way ahead runs slightly downhill and round a sharp corner as a path comes up from the south-east. ◄

There are now more views half right across the Medway valley.

Where the NDW turns north, the PW stays ahead gently up and down to reach Birling Hill. Go half left across the road to find the PW continuing. Soon there is a view (right) down to Paddlesworth Farm.

Among the cluster of farm buildings of **Paddlesworth Farm** is the tiny St Benedict's church, built within fifty years of Becket's death. After closing in 1678 it was used as a barn until restoration in the early 20th century. The building, now in the care of the Churches Conservation Trust, is open 10am to 4pm. A harvest festival service is held in October. The hamlet was known as Paddlesworth-cum-Dode after 1367 when it was decided to abandon nearby Dode Chapel which had lost its congregation to the Black Death. This joint parish is now part of Snodland where pilgrims might have been heading for a ferry.

Pass a stile (right) at a path to the farm and later a gate leading to a track to the farm. After a path junction the way turns slightly and the ground begins to fall. After a gate another track joins from the left. At **Ladds (or Lad's) Farm** (left) join a road by still keeping forward. Houses can be seen high on a cliff above a quarry. The road

STAGE 10 – WROTHAM TO HALLING

UPPER HALLING

Chapel Houses in Chapel Lane, at the crossroads' north-east corner, is the former St Lawrence Chapel dating from the 12th century. It had a chaplain until 1531 and closed in 1547. The chapel, divided into dwellings in the 19th century, is similar in size and age to the one at Paddlesworth. After the Reformation the redundant St Lawrence's was first used by drovers and travellers for overnight shelter. The former Black Boy pub on the south-east corner dates from at least 1788. Another former pub here is The Pilgrims Rest. In the 19th and early 20th centuries chalk and lime were taken down the hill by tramway to barges on the River Medway at Lower Halling.

Upper Halling's converted ancient chapel

narrows to climb steeply, passing Clements Farm (left) to reach **Upper Halling**.

At the crossroads by the former Black Boy pub (right) and former chapel (left), turn right into Meadow Crescent. Where the road ends follow the path by the houses (left) to a road on the far side. [Only to go directly down to

The Pilgrims' Way

Halfway down there is a clear view across to the growing Peters Village.

Peters Bridge on the edge of Halling and take the footpath on the right.] Still keep forward to go up Barn Meadow. Beyond the last house the way continues as the Plough Path. This is metalled and narrow as it runs for half a mile down the hill towards Halling. To the left is South Pit. ◂

At the bottom, rather than cross the usually busy road, go left. After 300 yards (0.2km) cross the bridge over the main road and follow the path down to a cemetery. Turn right and go over the railway to Lower Halling's main street. Halling church is to the right.

For Halling station

Turn left along the High Street to cross the railway bridge and turn right (¼ mile/0.4km).

STAGE 11
Halling to Aylesford

Start	Halling
Finish	Aylesford
Distance	4¾ miles (7.6km)
Time	2hrs
Maps	OS Explorer 148; Landranger 178
Refreshments	Pub at Halling; tea shop at Aylesford Priory
Public transport	Railway stations at Halling and Aylesford
Accommodation	Wouldham and Aylesford

This stage crosses the Medway valley where it cuts through the North Downs ridge. The old Pilgrims' Way crossed the River Medway by ferry at Halling or Snodland, although some pilgrims would have walked south to cross the ancient bridge at Aylesford. Belloc suggests that pilgrims waded across at Snodland to Burham while Cartwright goes for first Halling and then Snodland. The Halling ferry closed in 1963 so today the crossing is by the nearby road bridge. Once in the new Peters Village on the eastern bank there is the option of going north along the tidal River Medway to visit Rochester Cathedral before continuing south past the lonely Burham church towards Aylesford. The tidal reedbeds provide a habitat for birds wintering here.

From the station
At the main road go left over the bridge and follow the High Street to the church (¼ mile/0.4km).

From the High Street turn down Ferry Road by the church to pass the palace remains (right) and find the ferry steps ahead on the riverside. Turn right, upstream, to follow the riverside path. On the edge of Halling it turns sharp right, inland, across grass to join Howlsmere Close. Follow this road past Herying Close (right) to reach the High Street. Go left over the railway and left at the main road. On

HALLING

Halling is derived from a Saxon word meaning 'low place'. The much altered church, dating from the Norman period, has 12th-century wall paintings. The churchyard wall with lancet windows was the west end of the dining hall belonging to the Bishop of Rochester Gundulf's palace. It was built with Kentish Ragstone in 1086 and by the 13th century the palace had one of the best vineyards in the country. Thomas Becket's successor, Archbishop Richard, died at the house. St John Fisher was the last Bishop of Rochester to be in residence. In 1871 it became a lime and cement works with barges built in the village for carrying chalk downstream to the River Thames. The Cemex (Rugby Cement) factory quarried chalk nearby until 2010 when Blue Circle Cement helped to restore the palace remains.

Halling church from Wouldham bank

approaching the roundabout go left again to cross the railway a second time and then the River Medway (only the latest OS map will show Peters Bridge here) to reach Peters Village.

STAGE 11 – HALLING TO AYLESFORD

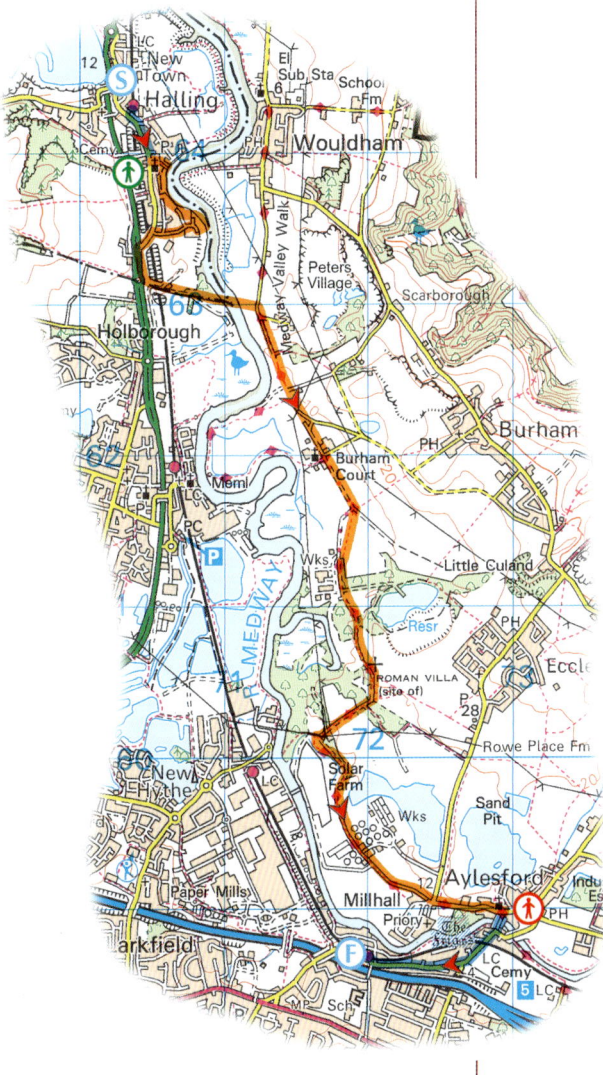

The Pilgrims' Way

Peters Village takes its name from William Peters who took over an existing lime works in 1857 and lived on site at Wouldham Hall until his death in 1867. Peters' Wouldham Hall Cement Works produced Portland Cement until 1926 while occupying the Wouldham Marshes riverside site between Wouldham to the north and the river bend above Burham to the south. The 18th-century Hall in the middle was demolished in 1960 and now the site is being developed as a 15,000-home garden village nearing completion. The river bridge, where a Bailey bridge stood during World War II, was completed in 2016.

At the roundabout in Peters Village, those visiting Rochester should turn left and follow Stage 11a.

After the village centre, the road is also called Village Road and comes close to the river (right).

The PW continues to the right to go along Village Road. ◄ Just after the water turns away west there is a path (right) leading to the ferry point opposite **Snodland**. However, the PW continues ahead while the road swings away. The path soon joins Old Church Road to reach the **lonely church at Burham**.

There are houses to the right (one sometimes selling ducks eggs) before the way is across flat open ground.

From Burham Church continue ahead over the junction on a hard surface road. ◄ At the road bend go ahead for a few yards to find a footpath running half right across a field as an off road short cut. In the corner go through a barrier and follow a short path. Go right and left to continue on the main path south which once crossed a brickworks.

Burham Brickworks was established by builder and developer Thomas Cubitt (see Stage 5) who erected four bottle kilns in 1850. Manufacturing his own bricks enabled him to guarantee good quality and meet deadlines. After his death five years later the operation was taken over by Burham Brick, Lime & Cement Co which expanded the site.

STAGE 11 – HALLING TO AYLESFORD

BURHAM

St Mary's is an isolated 12th-century church with two Norman fonts, the square one having been here longer. Outside the porch is an ancient yew tree. The church is open 10am to 3pm. Opposite the church gate is Burham Court dating from the 16th century. The village now lies on higher ground by the main road to the east. Pilgrims probably approached Burham from west and north, for a path at the side of the church runs directly to the ferry point opposite Snodland church. A stone at the ferry landing, placed largely at the instigation of writer Nigel Nicolson, claims that this was the point where the Romans crossed the Medway in AD43 when invading Britain.

Burham church porch

The way has a concrete surface as it double bends uphill to pass through a gateway. The path soon runs gently downhill alongside a solar farm seen through a high fence (right). Where the fence ends pass a pylon (right) and look to the left by low bollards for a narrow and easily missed path. This runs past another pylon (left) and soon bends left by a 'Danger Deep Water' notice.

The Pilgrims' Way

SNODLAND

The ferry house is in a corner of the churchyard. The Norman All Saints Church, which includes Roman tiles, was improved in successive centuries until the 14th century from when a wall painting survives. The tower has a priest's room with a fireplace on the first floor. The porch on the inland side was built in the 1460s. There are fragments of 15th-century glass and a 1965 window depicts pilgrims to Canterbury. The ferry, which once carried Peters' factory workers, ran until 1948. Snodland's market cross is now by the church door.

Stay on the narrow single file path round a sometimes flooded area. The path makes a sharp right turn before passing through a gateway by more low bollards. Soon the way has an old tarmac surface. Beyond a bike barrier the path widens to pass through a sewage farm. Keep forward on meeting a road at a bend. After a quarter of a mile (0.4km), 17th-century thatched barns, which include a tea shop, can be seen (right) in the grounds of **Aylesford Priory**. ◄

> The main priory entrance is to the right at a junction with the main road.

Known locally as The Friars, **Aylesford Priory** is England's oldest Carmelite priory having been founded by St Simon Stock in 1242. The community was expelled by Henry VIII in 1538 but returned in 1948 when 50 friars walked in procession along the road. A medieval courtyard (by a post box) includes the Pilgrims' Hall constructed in 1280 when it had a central fire for travellers to gather round. Over its door is a statue of Thomas Becket. The modern shrine chapel contains the skull of St Simon Stock. The mosaics, undertaken from 1966 to 1986 in the chapels, are by Adam Kossowski whose work is also seen in the Old Kent Road (see Stage 1a). The pottery was refounded in 1954 by David Leach, son of Bernard Leach. The priory is open 9am to 5pm (winter 4pm) but the public is welcome at evening prayer at 6.30pm; Sunday 6pm. Weekday Mass is at noon; Sunday 10.15am.

STAGE 11 – HALLING TO AYLESFORD

Continue ahead where the main road joins at the Priory entrance. There is a pavement on the left. Stay with this path when it leaves the road to pass the parish church on high ground. Turn right, downhill, to the High Street.

Adam Kossowski mosaics at Aylesford Priory

For Aylesford station
From the High Street cross the town bridge and follow the road ahead (¾ mile/1.2km). But to enjoy the river route with a view of the priory go right, having crossed the bridge, left at a car park, over a level crossing and right.

THE PILGRIMS' WAY

STAGE 11A
Peters Village to Rochester

Start	Peters Village Bridge
Finish	Rochester Cathedral
Distance	4½ miles (7.2km) (9 miles (14.4km) round trip)
Time	1¾hrs (3½hrs round trip)
Maps	OS Explorer 148; Landranger 178
Refreshments	Pubs at Wouldham, tearoom at Rochester Cathedral
Public transport	Bus at Wouldham and Rochester
Accommodation	Wouldham and Rochester

Rochester Cathedral was visited by pilgrims on the main London to Canterbury route. A number of those on the Pilgrims' Way would either have walked north through Cuxton to cross the River Medway at Rochester, or having crossed at Halling or Snodland, walked up the east bank from Wouldham. Rochester had its own saint, William of Perth, who was a pilgrim from Scotland. The location of his murder, just south of Rochester, suggests that he was on his way to joining the Pilgrims' Way. Visiting the cathedral and castle can easily fill a day. This is a nine-mile round walk into Rochester and back.

From Halling station
From the station approach go left over the bridge and follow the High Street to the church (¼ mile/0.4km). Then follow Stage 11 as far as the east end of Peters Village Bridge (1¼ miles/2km).

From the roundabout by the bridge in Peters Village go left to follow the road into **Wouldham**. Walk through the village to pass Wouldham Court Farm and reach the church. Beyond the next house (left) go left up a wide entrance. ◄

Beyond a second house and a gateway there is an information board by the river.

WOULDHAM

The church is at the village's north end where it must have appeared even more isolated when the village pond was on the south side. The church, which has Roman bricks in the 1058 Saxon work, was enlarged just before the first rector was appointed in 1283. The chancel was added in 1350 and the landmark tower followed in 1460. The riverside behind the church is known as Rectory Wharf. Walter Burke, the purser who cradled Lord Nelson as he was dying on HMS Victory in 1805, lived here and is buried (south side of path) in the churchyard. A local legend claims that Nelson was rowed from Chatham to visit Lady Hamilton here. Wouldham Court, opposite the lychgate, is a 16th-century building with a Georgian front.

Wouldham church

Bear right on a narrow path which follows the river. This is a permissive path along a field. After passing a waterworks (right) there is the first view of Cuxton church ahead. High on the hill overlooking the River Medway, Cuxton church is dedicated to St Michael and has a Norman nave and chancel. The tower is 14th-century. The path runs along the side of a field with a sudden view over the water before diving through a tunnel of growth. Afterwards the path is on a flood bank as it bears left.

THE PILGRIMS' WAY

Soon there is a first view of the dramatic Medway Bridges.

◀ Having turned north there is a handy seat by a turning inland. Continue along the bank. Houses in **North Halling**, below the cliff, can be seen opposite.

When the path is almost opposite Cuxton church, there is a picnic table on the inland side of the bank. Here a path runs inland from a footbridge to Starkeys, a 15th-century house in the trees.

> The first house on the remote wooded site, just above the Medway flood plain, **Starkeys** was built in 1360. The present building takes its name from Baron of the Exchequer Sir Humphrey Starkey who died in 1486 having rebuilt the house 15 years earlier.

From now on there is a view of Rochester's castle and cathedral seen through the high bridge ahead. The buildings inland, beyond Wouldham Marshes, are **Rings Hill Farm**. Where the bank ends at a fence go inland for just a few yards to find a narrow path by a white post.

Rochester Castle and Cathedral

Stage 11a – Peters Village to Rochester

Beyond is a track running past houseboats. Go through the kissing gate at the side of the main gate. Keep ahead and soon the way is passing under the Medway Bridges carrying the M2 and the channel tunnel high speed railway.

The path is briefly very close to the water before running round the back of a boatyard. On joining the Beacon Boatyard entrance approach keep forward. At the road go left on a firm path running along the edge of Baty's Marsh (left).

Originally called Borstal Marsh, the marshland of **Baty's Marsh** was renamed after Robert Baty, Director of the Royal Academy of Dramatic Art, who campaigned for the area to be made a nature reserve in 1987. The area, home to wading birds and wildlife, is one of the last salt marshes on the Medway not to have been drained.

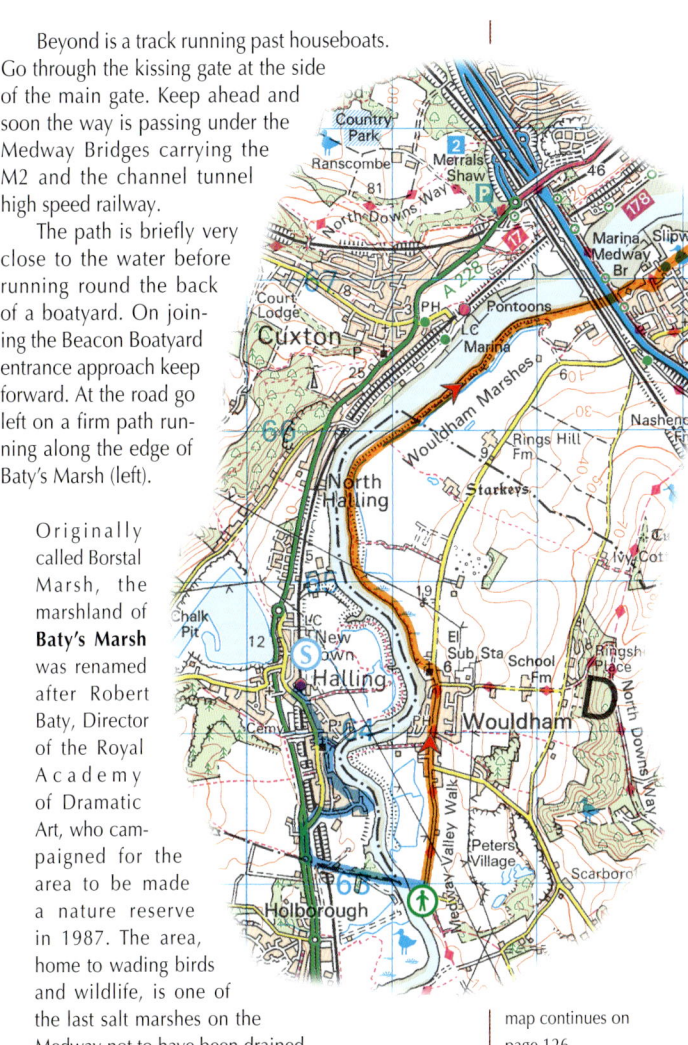

map continues on page 126

The Pilgrims' Way

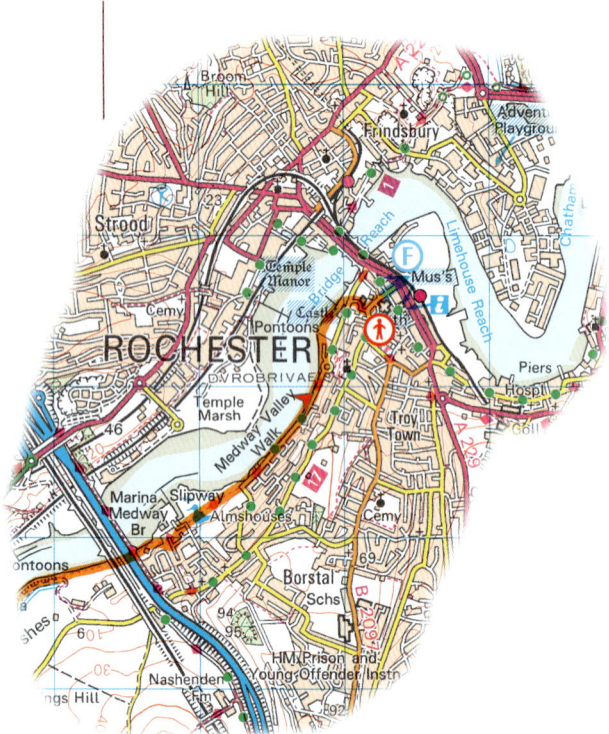

Ahead, beyond Rochester bridge, can be seen Frindsbury church high on a cliff above Strood.

There is a seat along the way and later two more with views before the path meets Esplanard, a riverside road. Keep forward on the pavement by the water. ◄ Where the road swings away, keep on the path by the water. At a sudden bend the waterside path is by grass.

Pass between the Rochester Cruising Club and its pier and after a few yards turn inland on a path leading directly to the road. Cross over to go up Baker's Walk. There is a narrow pavement on the left as the lane curves uphill to pass the castle. At a junction go left to reach the west door of the cathedral.

ROCHESTER CATHEDRAL

St William of Perth with his pilgrim shell and staff in a Rochester Cathedral window

The cathedral was founded by St Augustine in AD604. The present building dates from 1080 when Bishop Gundulf began building the nave and the Romanesque facade for a Benedictine community. This new cathedral was eventually consecrated in 1130 in the presence of Henry I who had encouraged Archbishop of Canterbury William of Corbeil to build the castle opposite. Its keep is the tallest in Europe. In 1215 the Magna Carta barons held out there against King John who was having second thoughts about his assent to the charter. By then the cathedral was a place of pilgrimage following the visit in 1201 by Scottish baker William from Perth who, on leaving Rochester for the new Becket shrine at Canterbury, was murdered. A miraculous healing of the person finding his body led to the baker being buried in the cathedral and canonised. St John Fisher, whose house is to the south of the cathedral, is depicted on the choir screen.

The cathedral shield is the cross of St Andrew, adopted here as patron saint 700 years before Scotland, with a shell recalling Scottish pilgrim St William. Bishop Walter of Rochester ordained Becket priest on the eve of consecration and enthronement as Archbishop. Chaucer, as a Kent magistrate, knew the city well and in *The Canterbury Tales* of 1387 has the monk tell his tale here. His story of the fickleness of fortune is said to have been prompted by the wheel of fortune painting which partly survives on the choir's north wall.

> To enter the cathedral by the traditional pilgrim doorway continue past the cathedral main door and through the arch to the high street. Go right and after a few yards right again up Black Boy Alley. A plaque in the ground marks the site of St William's Gate. Walk directly into the cathedral's north transept to go left up the pilgrim steps. St William's shrine was ahead in the north transept where he is depicted in a window.

To return to Wouldham, retrace the outward route. Turn left out of the cathedral west door and walk uphill. Turn right past the castle to follow Baker's Walk down to the grass by the River Medway. At the river go left to follow the water (right) to Wouldham church. Walk through the village to reach Peters Village roundabout and continue south on Stage 11.

STAGE 12
Aylesford to Harrietsham

Start	Aylesford
Finish	Harrietsham
Distance	11 miles (17.7km)
Time	4½hrs
Maps	OS Explorer 148 and 137; Landranger 178 and 189
Refreshments	Pubs at Aylesford, Boxley, Detling, Thurnham and Hollingbourne
Toilets	Aylesford High Street; petrol station by A229
Public transport	Railway stations at Aylesford, Thurnham (Bearsted station), Hollingbourne and Harrietsham
Accommodation	Aylesford and Thurnham

On this stage the path regains the ridge. A surprising amount of PW here continues to be a main metalled thoroughfare. Even in 1932 a walker complained of having to be 'pressed against a prickly hedge to obtain sanctuary from motor traffic' near Thurnham. A short stretch of the PW above Boxley is still subject to very heavy traffic but here there is an ancient alternative route taken by pilgrims. Travellers often used parallel paths to avoid mud or visit a nearby inn or church. At Boxley most would have dropped down to its abbey. Today it is recommended that walkers take the natural and ancient parallel path linking the churches of Boxley Abbey, Boxley village, Detling and Thurnham.

From Aylesford station
Turn left along the main road to reach the town bridge (¾ mile/1.2km). The alternative river route with a view of the priory goes left, left again over the level crossing and ahead to the river where a path runs to the right.

From the High Street pass the public toilets by Church Walk and go up Mount Pleasant. Soon there is a terrace of mid-Victorian cottages (left) and a medieval stone

The Pilgrims' Way

AYLESFORD

The 14th-century bridge, modified in 1824 to allow barges to pass beneath, is now traffic-free. The church, with a double nave out of alignment with the chancel, has a Norman tower which dominates the town. In the High Street is The Little Gem pub, built in 1106, and The Chequers Inn dating from the late Elizabethan period.

Aylesford Bridge and church

doorway (right) which has been moved from the church. At the end go left into Rochester Road. Take the pavement on the right to go uphill and right into **Pratling Street**. Pass a Waitrose depot and two turnings (right). There are now some houses (left). On approaching a row of cottages ahead take the right fork.

Pass the house (left) as an oast house comes into view ahead. The hard surface gives way to a rough track which runs between the former Great Cossington farm buildings. Where the track bears right, over a stream, go left. There is a gateway before this path swings right while

STAGE 12 – AYLESFORD TO HARRIETSHAM

the PW goes straight ahead to run along the side of a field (left). Beyond a kissing gate bear slightly right, up the field to another kissing gate where there is a view back across the Medway valley.
The path

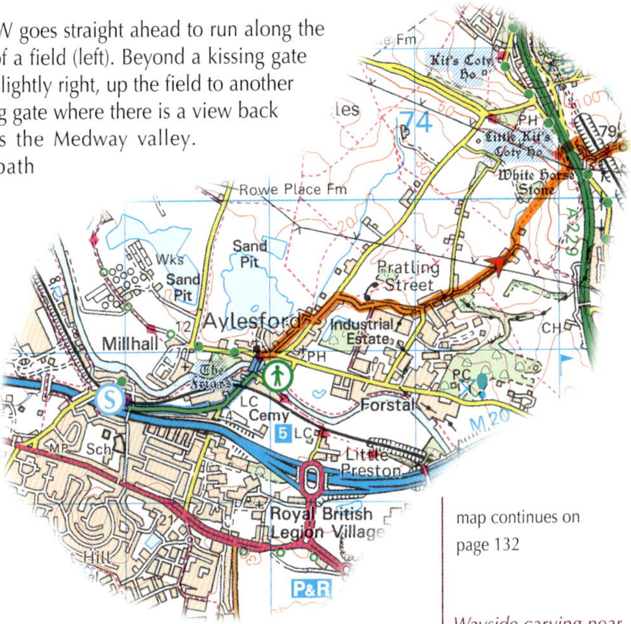

map continues on page 132

Wayside carving near White Horse Stone

continues forward to a hidden kissing gate in the trees (right). Bear left with the path through trees. Once in the open continue along the side (left) of a field. There is a signpost ahead.

On reaching a road go left to see the NDW joining (left). Keep ahead to go right, under the A229. The road rises as it curves round to the right to a junction of paths. To the right is the back of a petrol station with a shop. Do not go sharp left uphill but continue on the road to the left of a white building with a high green fence. Beyond a bend the way loses its hard surface to run above the channel tunnel high speed railway.

Go ahead up a hollow way. Soon there are steps (left) up to **White Horse Stone**, the remains of a Neolithic long barrow and part of the Medway Megaliths. A little further on more steps take the NDW away to the left. ▶ Stay

Just beyond the second steps, and easily missed, is a tree stump with a carving (above).

THE PILGRIMS' WAY

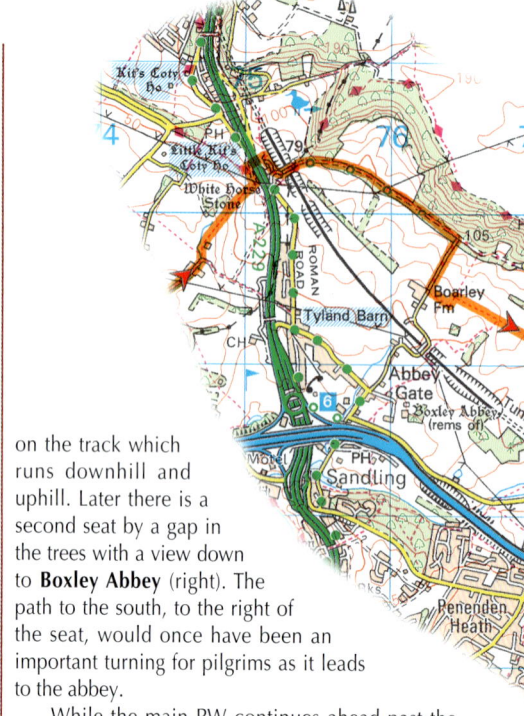

on the track which runs downhill and uphill. Later there is a second seat by a gap in the trees with a view down to **Boxley Abbey** (right). The path to the south, to the right of the seat, would once have been an important turning for pilgrims as it leads to the abbey.

While the main PW continues ahead past the seat, this guide takes the walker on the pilgrim path towards the abbey site to join the old parallel path linking the abbey to the next three churches. Just before the seat go right, on a narrow wooded and soon metalled path downhill to **Boarley Farm**.

To see the abbey gateway ruin go ahead through the farm to Boarley Lane and having crossed the railway take the footpath on the left. At a lane by cottages look left. On returning, cross the bridge again but take the footpath to the right. Turn right on meeting the path from Boarley Farm.

The route continues left between gates. The path runs alongside a hedge (right) and up a slope to a gap in a

STAGE 12 – AYLESFORD TO HARRIETSHAM

long line of trees. Bear left and shortly right to continue east. Again there is a short slope at the next boundary (where the return path from the abbey joins). Soon **Boxley** village can be seen ahead. On entering Barn Meadow, the way is along-

map continues on page 136

side trees (left) to join Forge Lane flanked by Anvil Cottage and Forge Cottage. At the end there is The Kings Arms (right) opposite Boxley Church.

Go over the stile left of the church lychgate and keep forward with the churchyard wall (right). Go over stiles

BOXLEY

'Boxley' is Saxon for 'box tree glade'. The parish church is a 13th-century building attached to the original Norman one which has become a large porch. Its dedication is All Saints & St Mary, the latter being added after the abbey of St Mary was closed. In the porch is a carved head of Edward II who stayed at the abbey. Tennyson's sister Cecilia Lushington is commemorated at the east end of the south aisle and buried in the churchyard. Her brother attended her wedding here. The Kings Arms, a successor to the abbey brewery, dates from Tudor times.

Boxley church

The remains of the Cistercian Abbey of St Mary in Boxley, once owned by Jane Austen's great uncle and still a private residence, was founded in 1146 and closed in 1538. The 186-foot-long guest house, which received pilgrims, survives having been used as a barn. Its long red roof can be seen from the viewpoint. Boxley's abbot was at Canterbury when Becket was murdered and helped to bury him. Edward II stayed on the way to Canterbury and in 1518 Cardinal Lorenzo Campeggio stopped on his way from Rome to London having visited Becket's shrine at Canterbury. His next night was at Otford. Around this time Archbishop Warham wrote to Cardinal Wolsey saying that Boxley was 'so holy a place where so many miracles might be showed'. The great attraction was in the abbey church where the rood screen featured moving figures operated off stage with wires. Another draw was a relic of St Andrew, once in the late 15th-century St Andrew's Chapel with integral priest's lodging which is just visible from Boarley Lane before the Grange Lane junction. Boarley Warren, the hill behind the viewpoint seat, was the abbey's rabbit warren.

STAGE 12 – AYLESFORD TO HARRIETSHAM

to cross two fields and through a kissing gate. At a track, continue in the same direction. There are usually open gates by another stile. Soon the way is through woodland to a gateway. Bear half right to pass a barn (left) and a house (right). The track runs uphill to pass two houses (left) by a T-junction. Look for a set back stile opposite. A path runs across a field to another stile below a bank. Go left with a fence and right, up steps to the usually very busy A249.

Turn left along a pavement to briefly rejoin the ancient Pilgrims' Way (left). Go ahead across the turning and past the mounting block to go up a passage leading to Jade's Crossing bridge. ▶ On the far side of the dual carriageway the ramp runs down to the road in **Detling**. Go round to the front of The Cock Horse.

> The dual carriageway was built in 1962. The footbridge, opened in 2002, is named after Jade Hobbs who with her grandmother was killed crossing the road in 2000.

> Norman St Martin's Church in **Detling**, at first a tiny chapel of ease within the parish of All Saints, Maidstone, was enlarged in 1887. Its unusual 14th-century lectern was probably rescued from Boxley Abbey when it closed. The Cock Horse, at the PW crossroads, dates from the early Tudor period.

Continue down The Street past the pub (right) and the Pilgrims' Way (left) to a junction with Hockers Lane (left). (The church is round the corner to the right behind Tithe Barn.) But the churches' link path continues on the left, at a telegraph pole, just before the junction. A fenced passage passes Broad View.

The enclosed narrow path runs in a straight line, and beyond the gardens is by an old orchard. Go through three kissing gates to continue in a straight line over two fields. Ahead is woodland surrounding **Thurnham's hidden church**. Half right there are sometimes high speed trains to be seen. After the third gate cross a metalled lane to find, set back, a gate leading to Thurnham churchyard.

> The motte and bailey castle above the village of **Thurnham** was built by the Normans in the early 12th century as a watchtower on the ancient route.

THE PILGRIMS' WAY

The church, although subject to some changes, also dates from this time. Its yew is even older. Thurnham Court on the south side is Tudor with a late Victorian extension.

Beyond the church (left) go through a gate leading to a path between a high wall and hedge. At the road there is a view of Thurnham Court beyond its gateway.

For Bearsted station
At the church entrance go right (south) along the road which runs under the M20 to the railway bridge (1 mile/1.6km).

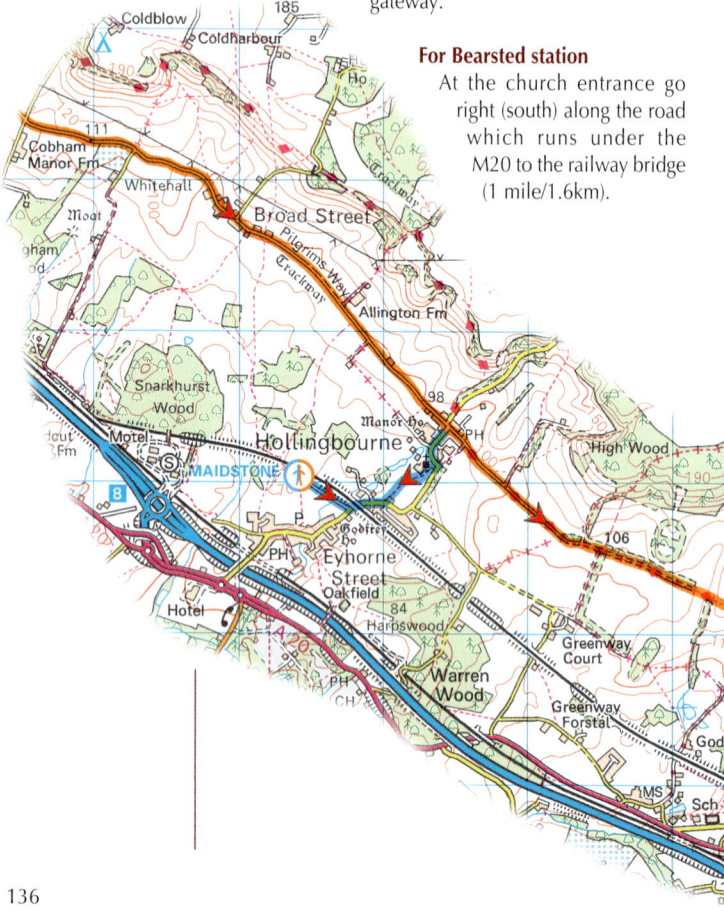

Stage 12 – Aylesford to Harrietsham

HOLLINGBOURNE

The name is derived from the hollies which once grew here and the water from springs in the hill. The Dirty Habit pub has an 18th-century front but is believed to date from the 13th century. It was once the Pilgrims Rest and the present name is derived from the clothing of monks who worked the monastic farmland and vineyard here. The manor was held by Canterbury Cathedral from before the Conquest. The present manor house, between the pub and the church, is Elizabethan. The church at the bottom of the hill was rebuilt in the 14th century but the walls retain a Norman thickness. The Culpeper Chapel, at the east of the north aisle, was originally dedicated to St James the Great. The village is divided by the railway with another pub south of the track.

From Bearsted station

Leave the station by the down side (from London) and follow the path and steps down to the road by the bridge. Go left along the road which runs under the M20 to Thurnham church (left; 1 mile/1.6km).

Turn left to a junction by a Victorian wall post box (left). Only continue ahead to visit the The Black Horse Inn.

To avoid the narrow road ahead go right at the post box. ▶ Walk to the far end passing a double oast house and former barn. Continue ahead as the lane narrows to a small gate. On the far side the metalled surface is resumed as the way bears left uphill to a road. Turn right onto the PW to head for Hollingbourne.

The lane has an always open white gate.

Soon go over the crossroads where Coldblow Lane (left) leads up to Cat's Mount (possibly a former walkers' shelter site). Ahead, the lane rises giving occasional panoramic views (right). Later it curves downhill to pass through **Broad Street**, a hamlet of former farmhouses. After Allington Farm (left) and white painted Little Allington, the road drops down to enter **Hollingbourne**. Opposite, beyond a blind bend (right), is The Dirty Habit pub.

For Hollingbourne station
Go downhill past the pub to the church. Take the path running past the west door to continue on a metalled way across a field. Go right, along the road, and right after the railway bridge (1 mile/1.6km).

The PW continues down the side of The Dirty Habit. After the houses, the way is across open country as it rises on the side of the valley. At a junction keep forward where the hard surface gives way to rough and the lane again rises. Ignore all turnings. Later the way is unfenced with open fields on one side as it runs gently up and down hills. On approaching Harrietsham, the path is wooded as it climbs to pass the Dutch House (left). As its drive joins from the left there is a wide path running downhill on the right leading directly to Harrietsham station.

To see the church take the station route but turn left at a metalled cross path.

> The **church in Harrietsham** may stand apart from the village to be near the PW. Its hidden Norman north tower has a room for a priest to stay overnight. The outstanding local Bethersden stone font is also Norman. The landmark west tower was rebuilt in 1479. A hidden lake to the south-east of the church, towards the station, is known as Pilgrims' Pool. The main village is south of the railway line.

For Harrietsham station
At the Dutch House entrance (left) go right, downhill. Cross a metalled road to continue downhill following a tree-lined footpath to the railway line (½ mile/0.8km). The way turns right to the platform entrance.

STAGE 13
Harrietsham to Boughton Lees

Start	Harrietsham
Finish	Boughton Lees green (near Wye)
Distance	11 miles (17.7km)
Time	4½hrs
Maps	OS Explorer 137; Landranger 189
Refreshments	Pubs at Harrietsham, Lenham and Boughton Lees; tea shops at Lenham, Charing, Perry Court and Wye
Toilets	Lenham and Charing (Old Ashford Road)
Public transport	Railway stations at Harrietsham, Lenham, Charing and Boughton Lees (Wye station)
Accommodation	Harrietsham and Lenham

This long stretch south of Harrietsham, much of which remains a road, has been used as a main route down the centuries. The principal stop prior to the Reformation was Charing where some of the Archbishop of Canterbury's palace survives alongside the church. James II came this way in December 1688, staying at an inn, while on his way to exile in France by way of Canterbury.

From Harrietsham station
Leave the station by the down side (from London) and follow the footpath by the line. This turns left uphill. At a metalled cross path, only go right for the church. Continue uphill on a wooded path which widens to reach the PW (½ mile/0.8km). Stage 13 continues to the right.

Shortly after the Dutch House, the PW crosses Stede Hill. ▶ Pass Marley Road (right) and a line of houses. At the bottom of the hill there is **Marley Court** (left) facing the former Marley Tile factory.

Continue ahead, pass Flint Lane (left) and where the road turns sharp right stay ahead as the PW becomes a

Soon after there is the figure of a monk sitting on a seat (left).

THE PILGRIMS' WAY

Harrietsham church

rough track again. At the top of the slope there can be a view of Lenham's church tower. Here the PW was given a sheltered north side with the planting of trees in 2000 to mark the Millennium. Soon the rough lane joins a metalled road above **Lenham**.

Only to reach Lenham go right, up steps to a path running down a field, then cross the main road to enter the village. The station is beyond the square.

For Lenham station
Take the footpath down to the main road and follow Faversham Road south to the square. Continue ahead along the High Street for the station approach just before the bridge (1 mile/1.6km).

From Lenham station and village
From the station road go left through the village centre. To avoid traffic, the return to the PW should be made by a footpath starting on the north side of the main road bypass. Cross the main road into Faversham Road

STAGE 13 – HARRIETSHAM TO BOUGHTON LEES

keeping on the
right passing Crossview Cottages. Keep
forward on the rising footpath which follows the brick
wall of Little Gaynes. Beyond a gate the path runs ahead
up a field. At the top go through a gate and after a few
yards turn right along the PW.

map continues on
page 144

LENHAM

The name comes from the infant River Len which feeds the Medway. In 1297 the church was badly damaged in an arson attack but part of that Norman building survives in the St Edmund Chapel. Most of the building dates from the 14th century. A painting of St Michael weighing souls has been on the south wall since about 1350. The vicar in the early 1800s was Edward Bridges, brother of Jane Austen's sister-in-law Elizabeth who lived at Godmersham (see Stage 14). Jane stayed at the vicarage where it is believed that the vicar unsuccessfully proposed to her. The Red Lion is 14th century while The Dog & Bear was built in 1602. Cornerhouse Café, with a rocking horse above the door, is a 15th-century house.

The PW continues ahead only briefly on the road. Be
ready to bear left after the cottages and just before the

The Pilgrims' Way

Lenham hillside cross

There is a seat at the base from where the view can be enjoyed.

next bend. The PW winds uphill to pass the second link path from Lenham (right).

Where the houses end, go ahead through a drop gate with an unusual 'No entry for carriages' sign. Soon the way passes a huge cross cut into the hill as a **war memorial** just a year after the one at Shoreham (see Stage 3a). ◄

Soon the way is in a strip of woodland as it runs up and down. After another drop gate continue on a road. Beyond a footpath (right), and just before a lay-by, the PW leaves the road on the right.

Again the path is partly wooded and runs up and down. Later the way passes a surprise line of houses and meets a road. Go left for a few yards and then right to find the PW continuing by the entrance to **Highbourne**. Ignore all turnings. Sometimes there is a good view (right) down to the Great Stour river below. The path is across open rolling country at **Cobham Farm**.

CHARING

The large village, which has several medieval houses with plaques along the high street, was a day's journey by horse from Canterbury. The manor was held by the Archbishop of Canterbury from the 8th century, and Charing Palace, built for overnight stays, was one of Thomas Becket's favourites. Henry VII was a guest on the eve of the Annunciation in 1507 and his son Henry VIII stopped there for the night in 1520 on his way to France having spent the previous night at Otford. The surviving barn was the dining hall and contains stone known to Becket. Charing was a pilgrimage site in its own right since the adjoining parish church displayed the block on which John the Baptist was beheaded. The relic, brought back from the Holy Land by Richard I just after Becket's murder, survived the Reformation only to be lost during a fire in 1590. The tower dates from around 1500 and so would have been seen by pilgrims during the last 30 years of pre-Reformation pilgrimage. St Richard of Chichester was rector in 1243.

Charing Palace Great Hall

The Pilgrims' Way

At **Hart Hill** the path swings left to a road opposite a house. Go right, downhill, for a short distance to find the way continuing on the left. The path is at first sheltered before Charing comes into view beyond the Gallops (right). At **Charing Hill** the path begins to rise before reaching a T-junction by Clock House (left). Twyford House is on the corner. Charing village is down the hill to the right

For Charing station
Turn right, downhill, ignoring all turnings (¾ mile/1.2km).

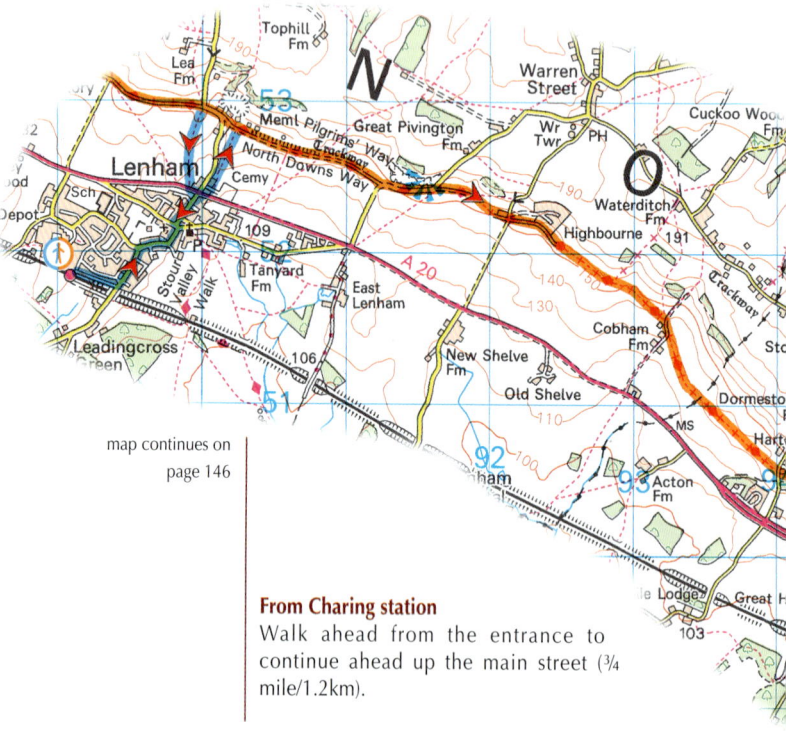

map continues on page 146

From Charing station
Walk ahead from the entrance to continue ahead up the main street (¾ mile/1.2km).

Stage 13 – Harrietsham to Boughton Lees

The PW continues past Twyford House (right) and Clock House (left) to meet a main road by Reeves Cottage (left). Cross the road and go left for a short distance to turn right. Here the PW continues as a metalled road which rapidly leaves houses behind. Soon there is Lone Park Farm (left) and a view back to Charing church tower. Beyond Toll Lane (right) there is a brief view behind of a windmill on Charing Hill. After Burnt House Farm (left) the road double bends to run uphill towards Charing Quarry. Bear half right.

Here the way becomes a typical PW track as it runs along the edge of woodland on the side of the hill with a view to the right. ▶ After passing through thicker woodland there is Wychling Over cottage (right). Continue forward keeping left at the fork. Round the corner the track joins a metalled road.

Just beyond a seat there is an entrance to Westwell Downs.

Soon after Flint Cottage (left) there is a barrier entrance to a footpath (right; only for village) leading down to a corner of **Westwell**. The closed pub is ahead down the village street with the church to the right.

Canterbury Cathedral funded the unusually spacious 13th-century church at **Westwell** which has some original glass in a Jesse window. A vineyard here was tended by Canterbury monks. The Wheel Inn, which opened about 1839, is also a food shop.

THE PILGRIMS' WAY

The line of the ancient way may have been over to the right.

The PW continues past the buildings clustered around **Dunn Street Farm** and **campsite**. At the T-junction go ahead to a stile. Bear left for a short distance and then right on a wide path down the field in **Eastwell Park**. ◄

Soon the path is by the narrow Skeate's Wood (right). The way rises and as farm buildings appear in the distance a notice warns 'No entrance to public'. Here go right to double bend through the wood and continue eastwards on the far side. There are the remains of a redundant stile which now serves as a seat. Where the trees end bear only slightly right to continue across the field. Over to the left is the large **Home Farm** mansion.

The path meets a metalled park road at a junction. Go forward. After a few yards there is a narrow kissing gate (right) where a path leads to

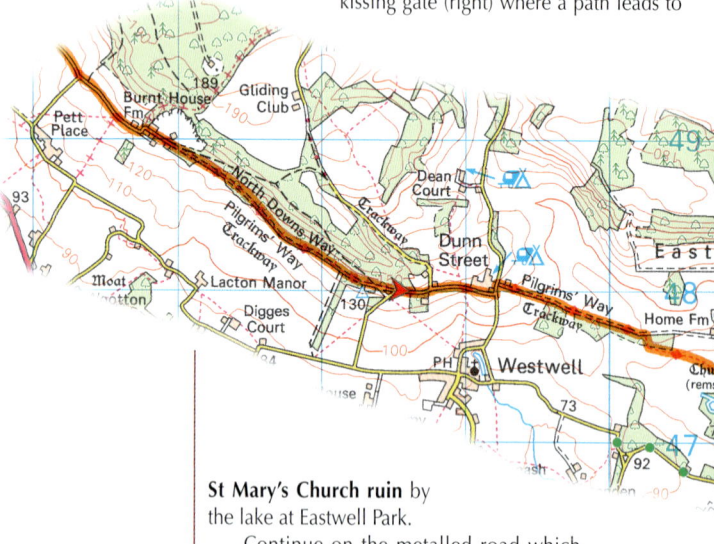

St Mary's Church ruin by the lake at Eastwell Park.

Continue on the metalled road which climbs to give a view over the lake (right). At a junction near Eastwell Manor keep forward through a kissing gate. Follow a fence (right) which passes a kissing gate where signposts indicate that this path is part of the Inverness to Nice E2 Grande Randonnée. After a lonely tree stump, a

Stage 13 – Harrietsham to Boughton Lees

EASTWELL

Only the 15th-century tower of St Mary's Church survives intact. A World War II bomb damaged the building and in 1951 the roof collapsed. An inscription on a tomb now open to the elements indicates that it may be that of Richard Plantagenet who is said to have last seen his father Richard III in a tent on the eve of the Battle of Bosworth and who in later life worked as a gardener at Eastwell Manor. The hidden Lake House next to the church dates from about 1300 and was probably the original manor house. The lake was dug in the 19th century.

The Tudor period Eastwell Manor, on the hill to the east, had just been largely rebuilt when Jane Austen visited George and Lady Elizabeth Hatton in 1805. Later in the century it was the home of Queen Victoria's son Prince Alfred. In 1926 the house was again rebuilt in the style of an Elizabethan mansion and is now a hotel.

finger post points half left downhill to a kissing gate by the hotel drive. Go right for a few yards and then left to a

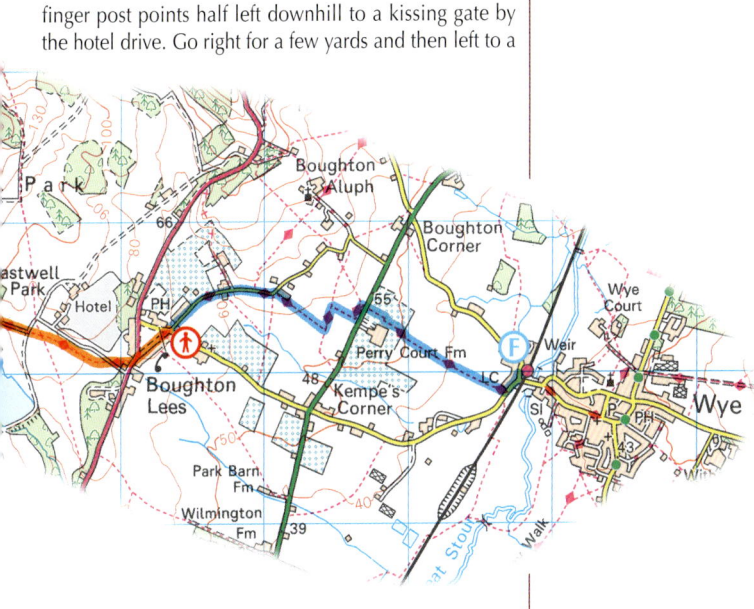

set back kissing gate. Walk diagonally across the field to another kissing gate in the corner next to St Christopher's church at Boughton Lees.

Cross the road with care to follow the right (east) side of the green which has a war memorial cross in the middle. The Flying Horse Inn is on the north side.

For Wye station

Take the Pilgrims' Way lane in the north-east corner of the green at the start of the next stage. Where the NDW divides and the PW leaves the lane, keep ahead. At the bend go through a kissing gate (right) and turn left. Go right with the field boundary and left at the next corner. At the third corner leave the boundary (left) by turning right and heading across the field. On the far side turn left to follow the hedge (right) for a short distance to a gap. Cross the main road to a gate and enter **Perry Court Farm**. The path runs alongside an apple orchard. At a junction, with the farmyard and tea room to the right, go ahead on the wide track but where this bears right keep ahead on the narrow path. This double bends before continuing east. Cross a field and keep forward. At a road go left for the level crossing and station (1½ miles/2.4km).

STAGE 14
Boughton Lees to Chilham

Start	Boughton Lees green
Finish	Chilham
Distance	6 miles (9.6km)
Time	2¼hrs
Maps	OS Explorer 137; Landranger 189
Refreshments	Pub at Boughton Lees; tea shop at Perry Court, Wye
Public transport	Railway stations at Boughton Lees (Wye) and Chilham
Accommodation	Boughton Lees

According to the OS map the PW runs close to Wye, but this is not confirmed by the great Victorian experts nor local landmarks. The NDW at first keeps largely to the probable route. However, the PW must later join a lower road to enter Chilham by way of Godmersham, known to pilgrims and Jane Austen.

From Wye station
Leave Wye station on the west side of the level crossing to go left into Harville Road. Where the houses end go right, onto a footpath. This runs through a meadow to a stile, across a field to another stile and along an enclosed path. At the far end this bends right and left to join a track at **Perry Court Farm**. At a junction (tea room in the farmyard, left) keep forward to reach a gate at a main road. Cross over and enter a field. At once go left along the hedge (left). On reaching a blocked gate in the hedge go sharp right across the field. At a field corner turn left and at the second go right. Keep by the field edge (right) and at the far end bear left to a kissing gate. Turn left on a lane called Pilgrims Way which bends. Look for a footpath on the right before the lane drops down (1½ miles/2.4km).

BOUGHTON LEES

St Christopher's, a 15th-century secular building, became a church in 1952 for use in winter due to lack of heating at Boughton Aluph church. The Flying Horse Inn with Dering windows dates from the 17th century. The round top windows are mostly seen in nearby Pluckley, England's allegedly most haunted village, and recall Sir Edward Dering who escaped through a similar window during the Civil War.

The Flying Horse Inn at Boughton Lees from the green

Take the Pilgrims' Way in the north-east corner of the green by Wye Road (right). Pass a line of houses. At Malthouse Farm and Brewhouse Lane (left) continue ahead up the slight hill to a gap on the left.

Stay on the lane to follow the NDW link to Wye station.

STAGE 14 – BOUGHTON LEES TO CHILHAM

The PW continues up a slope (left) to follow a narrow path which soon runs through a tunnel of trees. After a double bend the way is on a wooded bank. On entering a field, the tower of **Boughton Aluph church** can be seen ahead. Shortly before the end of the field go through a kissing gate (right) into a long field with a tree in the middle. Halfway down, a gate (left) leads into the churchyard.

The name **Boughton Aluph** (pronounced Borton Aluff) comes from 13th-century lord of the manor Aluphus de Boctune who began the replacement of the Saxon church. The north transept has a Trinity wall painting from about 1350. The porch with fireplace has given rise to a suggestion that pilgrims gathered here to warm themselves before going ahead in groups for safety as they approached the woods at

map continues on page 154

151

The Pilgrims' Way

GODMERSHAM

The tower of St Lawrence Church was built about 1070 while the nave and chancel are mainly 13th century. Victorian restoration by William Butterfield has resulted in the west door, used by Jane Austen when staying at Godmersham Park, being blocked up. Jane's brother Edward Knight is commemorated with a window. In the chancel is a stone plaque depicting an archbishop and thought to have been part of Thomas Becket's shrine at Canterbury. Godmersham Park Heritage Centre, alongside the churchyard, is open on the first Sunday of the month April to October, 9am to 5pm, and there is an admission charge.

Godmersham Park belonged to Canterbury Cathedral. The present mansion, now the Association of British Dispensing Opticians College, was built in 1732 on the site of a Tudor house and inherited by Edward Knight through his wife Elizabeth. (The legacy included Chawton Manor; see Stage 2.) Jane visited often from 1794 to 1813 and here worked on *Pride and Prejudice* and *Mansfield Park*, which feature Godmersham, and *Emma*. The £10 bank note design depicts Jane Austen with Godmersham Park in the background. Elizabeth's brother Edward Bridges, vicar of Lenham (see Stage 13), often visited with his wife.

Godmersham Park

STAGE 14 – BOUGHTON LEES TO CHILHAM

Seats in Boughton Aluph churchyard

Godmersham. The church is used for worship in the summer and is a venue for the Stour Music Festival. Boughton Court on the north side has a 14th-century undercroft and Dering windows.

On reaching the road at the kissing gate, or churchyard gateway, go over a stile to the left of the holly tree opposite. Soon there is a fence on the left. At a gate go left over a stile and then right to follow a path ahead downhill and then uphill. At a field corner go ahead just inside a hedge. The narrow path bends left to pass a stile (left) before turning right. At the lane go ahead on a track leading to **Soakham Farm**. ▶

There is a magnificent view to the right over the Stour Valley.

The way runs downhill and through a farmyard. Where the concrete ends keep forward to a gate. A track double bends uphill before bearing left. The path bends to the right along the edge of King's Wood (right). Go through a high deer gate to reach a junction. Go right and at a divide, with Pilgrims' Way sign, bear left. Keep to the main track as it gently descends and left again at

The Pilgrims' Way

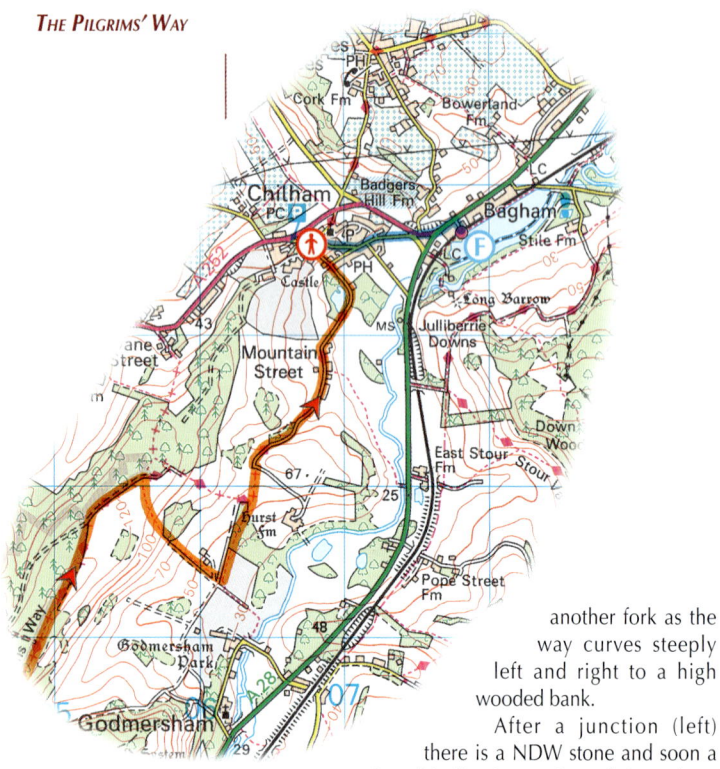

another fork as the way curves steeply left and right to a high wooded bank.

After a junction (left) there is a NDW stone and soon a board indicating a view of Canterbury Cathedral. Almost 0.5 miles further on there is a low brick deer wall (right). Leave the NDW by going right through the tall narrow gate (right).

Cross the field to a stile. In the hilltop meadow follow the tall yellow posts downhill to a stile by a gate. A straight path ahead affords a view down to Godmersham House and ahead to a summerhouse said to have been used by Jane Austen. Pass a house to reach an estate track junction. (Only to visit the church go ahead to gates, bear right to the main gateway by a lodge and turn right on a road.) The PW is left onto a hedged way. This is the beginning of **Mountain Street**, and still the old Canterbury main road, leading to The Square in Chilham.

Soon the way is in a field alongside a wood. In the corner keep forward to a high gate. An ancient wooded lane runs ahead, and only beyond another gate, at a junction, does it become metalled. After a hamlet there is the castle wall (left) which when built in 1728 caused the road to be slightly diverted. A gate and then brief railing gives a glimpse of the castle and lake. Keep forward at a junction past Elephant House (left) and up School Hill to the hilltop village. ▶ The PW runs across The Square and past the White Horse Inn into the churchyard.

Opposite, at the Chilham Castle gate, is a modern sculpture of pilgrims.

Chilham Castle was built by Henry II in 1171, the year after Becket's death. The adjoining building which is the residence was completed in 1616. Here Jane Austen attended a ball and dinners hosted by James Wildman. For a time her niece Fanny Knight from Godmersham was about to marry him. Later he had to sell the castle after losing his income from a plantation, having backed the abolition of slavery promoted by his friend William Wilberforce. The family has a memorial by Francis Chantrey in the church which dates from the Norman period but stands on 7th-century foundations. The tower was added in 1534 just before Henry VIII stopped pilgrimage.

For Chilham station
From The Square walk down The Street to The Woolpack (right). Bear left to the main road. Turn right along the main road to find the turning to the station (right) opposite The Old Alma Inn (¾ mile/1.2km).

STAGE 15
Chilham to Canterbury

Start	Chilham Church
Finish	Canterbury Cathedral
Distance	7 miles (11.2km)
Time	2½hrs
Maps	OS Explorer 137 and 150; Landranger 179
Refreshment	Pubs at Chilham, Harbledown and Canterbury; tea shops at Chilham and Canterbury
Public transport	Railway stations at Chilham and Canterbury
Accommodation	Chilham and Canterbury

The PW between Chilham and Chartham Hatch probably ran at first briefly near the River Stour although a clear route has never been agreed for this stretch by the early writers or the OS. Travellers may have entered Chartham for refreshment at The Artichoke inn or to see the church which has a brass of Sir Robert de Septvans, who knew Becket. But the NDW route is the most realistic as far as the higher Chartham Hatch. This stage's climax is Harbledown where the Winchester and London via Rochester routes come together as Canterbury Cathedral is glimpsed for the first time.

From Chilham station

Turn left at the main road, go left into Bagham Road and right at The Woolpack up The Street to the village square (¾ mile/1.2km).

The PW runs ahead down the side of the White Horse and past the church door. At once leave the main path to keep ahead down a footpath and where it divides keep left. Join the bottom of Church Hill and keep ahead to a main road. Cross over to go ahead into Long Hill and over a second junction. Still keep ahead up Long Hill

Stage 15 – Chilham to Canterbury

which climbs to pass the first of many orchards and reach a junction in **Old Wives Lees**.

> In 1610 **Old Wives Lees** was known as Old Wyves Lease. At the start of the 20th century there were about 35 dwellings and now there are about 240 houses. The hamlet falls within the Chilham parish. The shop, pub and post office have closed.

The Star Inn is a few yards to the left. The PW continues half right along Lower Lees Road, by the post box and signed to Shalmsford Street.

At the far end are two oast houses. Just beyond here go left and at the next junction turn right for just a few yards. Take the footpath on the left which runs straight ahead gently downhill. At first it is lined by carefully planted trees screening the orchards. At the bottom of the hill cross the field. To the right is a forest of hop poles.

On the far side go right, along a track, and just past a gate go left up a steep track lined by trees (right). At the top the path enters a

map continues on page 160

The Pilgrims' Way

The White Horse at Chilham

There are three oasts over to the left beyond the apple trees.

field and bends to run down a slope. At the corner go left. Ignore the first gap in the hedge. Keep along the field boundary (right) for 190 yards (175 metres) to cross a (maybe) broken stile (right).

Go ahead down the side of a sloping orchard. Soon there are apple trees on both sides and later the path kinks a little to the right. At the bottom keep forward as the way passes pickers' caravans and bears right. The track is downhill with a view of oast houses at the large farm site. Go left on the hard surface road passing under the railway. ◀

Just before a driveway go right, not up the track but a footpath. At first there is a fence (left) as the way climbs in the trees. Sometimes the track to the right can be seen. At the top go forward to turn left along a concrete farm road. A white house can be seen in the distance. The road bears round to the right to pass a lonely grave (which may be visible left) and a seat at a viewpoint.

Continue along the way passing the white cottage (right). Where the way divides do not go towards the oast houses and **radio mast** but left. There is a high hedge (right) before the road meets a village road at a bend in **Chartham Hatch**.

> **'Hatch'** means gap in the forest and Chartham Hatch consisted of scattered cottages until the 20th century when a hamlet grew. The Chapter Arms, a farmhouse that was a pub from 1862 to 2017, takes its name from its former owner, the Canterbury Cathedral Dean and Chapter. The main village of Chartham is in the valley.

On joining the road at Chartham Hatch keep ahead. Pass the 18th-century Mount Cottages and at a junction bear right into Town Lane.

Continue ahead to a crossroads by the village hall (left). There is a handy seat provided by the parish council (right) at the entrance to Bigbury Road opposite. Go ahead up this road which is signed Pilgrims Way. Soon the NDW passes across the road. On leaving the houses, the road runs through Highfield Wood. Later the way imperceptibly passes across **Bigbury earthwork**. At a bend keep forward along the narrower road marked 'Pilgrims Way' and passing through a brief tunnel of trees.

Soon there is a view over part of Canterbury just before the lane drops downhill past Bigbury Oast (right). At a junction go left and at once right between posts. Go over the stile on the left and walk just slightly left to follow a field boundary (right). The field rises and falls to a stile at a road. The NDW joins opposite.

Go right to cross the bridge over the main road. As the NDW leaves to the right keep ahead on the road running towards **Harbledown**. The bottom of the hill is on the line of Watling Street, the Roman road from London also used by pilgrims.

The road rises to pass Kent College (right) before going downhill again. At the bottom is the village sign (right) and a post box (left). ▶ To view St Thomas' Well, go right, opposite the post box on a signed path to pass a barn (left). Turn left into St Nicholas Hospital grounds

St Nicholas Hospital tower can be seen ahead above the trees.

The Pilgrims' Way

to find the well after a few yards on the left of the rising entrance. Walkers may continue ahead to the church and almshouses.

After passing the Harbledown village sign the road bends right, uphill. Steps (right) lead up to an archway entrance to St Nicholas.

HARBLEDOWN

This is the last stop for Chaucer's pilgrims where, since the cook is too tired or drunk to tell a tale, the Manciple steps forward. His prologue explains that the village name means 'bob up and down' in reference to the hill. Here on 12 July 1174 Henry II dismounted to begin his walk of penance into Canterbury. St Nicholas Hospital was founded for the care of lepers by Archbishop Lanfranc in 1087, the year the body of St Nicholas was brought from Myra in Turkey to Bari in Italy. The present almshouses were erected in 1674 and restored in 1840. St Thomas' Well in the grounds is decorated with the feathers of the Black Prince who restored it. Pilgrims calling here used to be able to see Becket's slipper. St Michael & All Angels church higher up the hill dates from 1050.

Stay on the left-hand side of the road to continue up Church Hill past the Coach & Horses (left). The path climbs steeply above the road to be level with the village church.

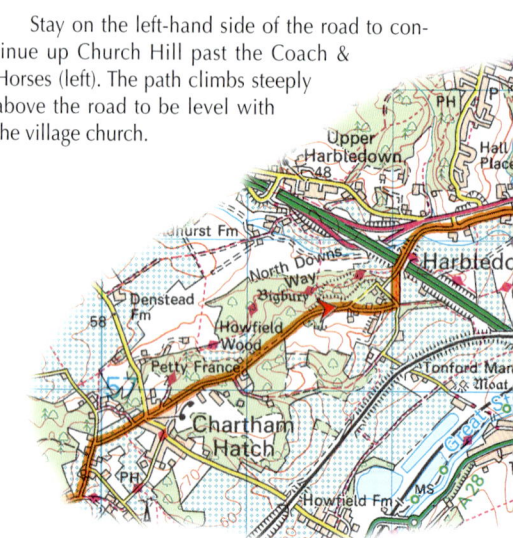

Stage 15 – Chilham to Canterbury

Beyond a crossroads descend Summer Hill by walking on the right-hand side to see the first view of Canterbury Cathedral. ▶ On joining the modern main road the view improves. At the roundabout, where there is a pedestrian underpass on the far side, go left into London Road to reach St Dunstan's church at the end.

The bell tower would have been seen from the 1490s.

St Dunstan's church, the final church before the city, was founded just after the Conquest by Archbishop Lanfranc and dedicated to his predecessor. Here Henry II changed into a woollen pilgrim shirt and removed his boots to continue his walk barefoot. Over the centuries other pilgrims have made this church their last stop before arriving at Becket's shrine in the cathedral. The head of St Thomas More, having been exhibited on London Bridge, was buried in the church's Roper Chapel by his daughter Margaret Roper who lived nearby. The anniversary of his martyrdom in 1535 is marked here every year on 6 July, the eve of the Translation of St Thomas Becket.

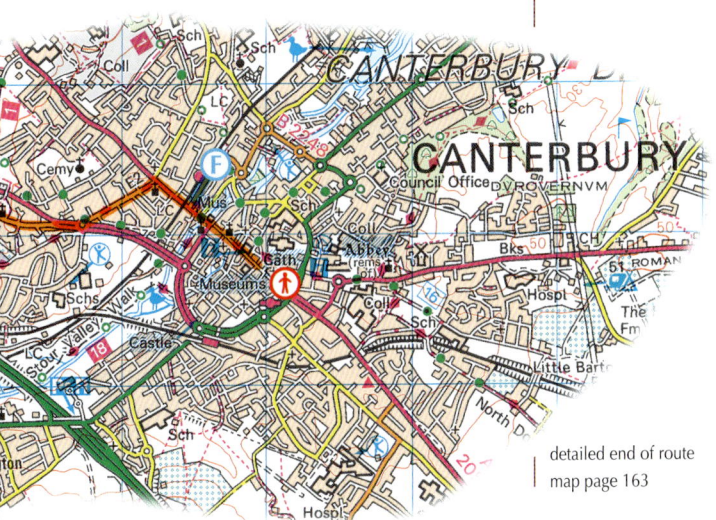

detailed end of route map page 163

THE PILGRIMS' WAY

St Dunstan's church

Turn right along St Dunstan's Street to pass the Roper Gate (left) entrance to the home of Thomas More's daughter. Cross the level crossing, pass Station Road West leading to Canterbury West station, and the very early 14th-century Falstaff Hotel (left) which accommodated pilgrims arriving after the gates ahead were shut. Keep through the city's west gate, and forward along St Peter's Street which leads into the High Street. Here the road passes the Eastbridge Hospital of St Thomas the Martyr (right) which spans part of the River Stour.

STAGE 15 – CHILHAM TO CANTERBURY

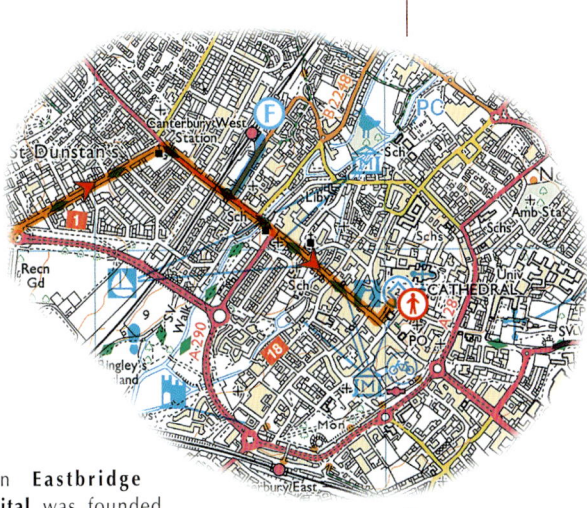

When **Eastbridge Hospital** was founded in 1180, with Becket's nephew Ralph as the master, it provided accommodation for poor pilgrims. Opposite is ASK, with a plaque recording the house being the site of a mill granted by Henry II to Becket's sister Rohesia during his 1174 penitential visit.

map scale 1:25,000

On reaching Mercery Lane (left) go left between a stone frontage shop, the former Chequers of the Hope pilgrim inn, and Pret A Manger. Mercery Lane leads directly to the Buttermarket and cathedral gateway. Go ahead through Christ Church Gate for the cathedral. ▶

For St Thomas of Canterbury church, where Becket relics are displayed, go right, before the gate along Burgate.

Those with a PW passport will normally be admitted free.

The **Martyrs Chapel** in St Thomas of Canterbury Church, Burgate, has three Becket relics probably taken from the body when it was placed in the cathedral shrine in 1220. Also displayed are vestments worn by Blessed Oscar Romero.

The Pilgrims' Way

CANTERBURY CATHEDRAL

This is the seat of the Primate of All England and until 1540 also the priory church for a Benedictine community. The building known to Becket had opened in 1077 and been enlarged by St Anselm. Pilgrims walked through the Quire and past St Augustine's Chair to approach Becket's shrine. Today a single candle burns on the site. This is Trinity Chapel, where Becket had celebrated his first Mass, and in the vaulting above can be seen the boss from which a pulley was suspended to raise the cover over the tomb. Restored 13th-century windows depict early pilgrims who came for healing, including two crippled sisters from Boxley along with others from Rochester, Reading, Winchester and Cologne. Beyond is the Corona Chapel which contained a fragment of Becket's broken skull. The site of the murder is in the north transept where in 1982 Pope St John Paul and Archbishop Robert Runcie of Canterbury prayed together. In 1935 the premiere of TS Eliot's *Murder in the Cathedral* was staged in the Chapter House off the cloister.

Canterbury Cathedral from the Archbishop's Palace

LONDON TO CANTERBURY

The path to Shoreham (Stage 3a)

The Pilgrims' Way

STAGE 1A
Southwark to Shooters Hill

Start	Southwark Cathedral
Finish	The Bull, Shooters Hill
Distance	8½ miles (13.6km)
Time	4hrs
Maps	OS Explorer 173, 161 and 162; Landranger 177
Refreshments	Pubs at Southwark, Old Kent Road and Blackheath
Public transport	Railway stations at Southwark (London Bridge station), Deptford Bridge, Blackheath and Woolwich Arsenal; bus at Shooters Hill
Accommodation	Hotels in Southwark, Deptford Bridge and Blackheath

From London Bridge there is a view through Tower Bridge to Shooters Hill at the end of this section. There are plenty of buses to speed the urban journey but the authentic route is best appreciated on foot. Pilgrim records (passports) are available at Southwark Cathedral.

Those starting at nearby St George's Cathedral (Roman Catholic) should follow the 1 mile Romero Way to Southwark Cathedral (Anglican); see page 195.

From London Bridge Underground station
Take the Borough Market exit and turn right to walk down Bedale Street to the cathedral (250 yards/0.2km).

Southwark Cathedral lies in Southwark's ancient hub known as The Borough. Borough Market, once selling mainly fruit and vegetables from Kent, moved next to the cathedral from the high street in 1756. In Borough High Street there is the 17th-century George Inn almost next to Talbot Yard, site of the Tabard inn mentioned in *The Canterbury Tales* by Geoffrey Chaucer and also frequented by William Shakespeare. Today the great landmark is

STAGE 1A – SOUTHWARK TO SHOOTERS HILL

SOUTHWARK CATHEDRAL

The cathedral was founded as a minster about 860, became an Augustinian priory in 1106, a collegiate parish church in 1539 and a cathedral in 1905. Thomas Becket visited from Canterbury just weeks before his murder. Afterwards the monks rededicated their infirmary which survives as St Thomas' Hospital. A resident in old age was Geoffrey Chaucer's friend the poet John Gower who has a magnificent tomb in the north aisle where he is depicted resting his head on his books. These inspired William Shakespeare, whose brother Edmund is buried between the choir stalls. The baptism certificate of their Stratford friends' child, John Harvard, of American university fame, is displayed nearby. Their contemporary, Bishop Lancelot Andrewes, is buried by the high altar. Opposite the Shakespeare window is the Chaucer window showing pilgrims leaving the Tabard inn. The east end screen, a copy of Winchester's, was erected in 1520: in the second row of figures are St Swithun (second from left) and St Thomas Becket (third from left). Outside, a herb garden contains apothecary roses and plants once used for cooking, medicine, brewing, strewing, fumigation and dyeing in the hospital.

Chaucer's friend John Gower resting on his books

The Pilgrims' Way

The Shard which rises over a thousand feet above the capital. The 95-storey glass wall structure, completed in 2013, is seen from the PW in Surrey.

Leave the cathedral by walking along Cathedral Street. Turn right into covered Borough Market and then left along Stoney Street. This leads to Southwark Street. Cross to the HSBC building and then Borough High Street. Turn right to pass The George (left) and Talbot Yard. At St George's Church turn left to cross the piazza at the side.

Henry V stopped at **St George's Church** on his way back from victory at the Battle of Agincourt having given thanks at Becket's Canterbury

168

STAGE 1A – SOUTHWARK TO SHOOTERS HILL

shrine. In *Little Dorrit* Charles Dickens depicts Amy sleeping in front of the vestry fireplace using the burial register as a pillow. Until cleared, the crypt held the

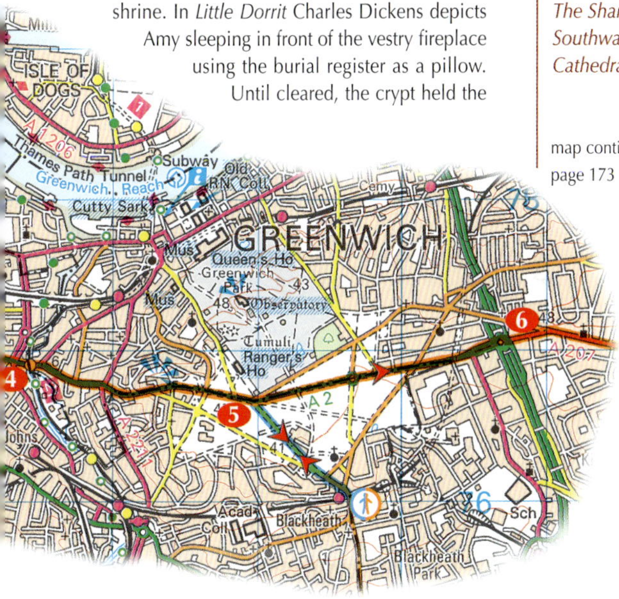

The Shard and Southwark Cathedral tower

map continues on page 173

THE PILGRIMS' WAY

bodies of Nahum Tate who wrote 'While Shepherds Watched their Flocks by Night' and Andrew Stoney of 'stoney broke' fame. The church is the capital's oldest dedicated to England's patron saint. The country's oldest is on the PW in Wrotham.

Walk between the church (right) and the churchyard (left) to cross Long Lane and follow Tabard Street, formerly Kent Street and the ancient Roman Watling Street. The Royal Oak pub is on the right before the road crosses Pilgrimage Street and runs alongside Tabard Gardens. ◄ Later there are flats named after places on the Pilgrims' Way including Chilham near Canterbury. At the far end, the former Hartley's jam factory can be seen down Prioress Walk (left). Ahead is the Bricklayers Arms roundabout (**1**).

Turn round here to see St George's Church framed by the street.

The **Bricklayers Arms roundabout** at the start of the long road recalls a coaching inn which was rebuilt in the 19th century and survived on the eastern corner of Tower Bridge Road until demolished for the 1970 flyover. The sign depicted the Tylers and Bricklayers livery company arms. The name became famous after 1844 when a railway terminus opened here. Its sidings were used until 1981.

OLD KENT ROAD

The main road, famous as the cheapest property on the London Monopoly board, is gradually being greened again in a plan to highlight its history. Becket came up this road on his way to Southwark. The first half mile to St Thomas a Watering offers great historic interest. On the north side at 155 is a surviving house built in 1800 as the home and office of architect Michael Searles who built some of the terrace houses in the street, now partly hidden by shops covering their gardens. On the south side in 1793 he developed Surrey Square on a market garden. Born in one of the houses was artist Samuel Palmer whose home is passed on the route in Kent. Searles' famous work is found later at Blackheath.

STAGE 1A – SOUTHWARK TO SHOOTERS HILL

THE THOMAS A BECKET PUB

The Lord Mayor of London and City aldermen came here to welcome visitors such as Henry V in 1415 and Charles II at the Restoration in 1660. A stone set into the nearby old fire station indicates the former limit of the City of London's liberty. The pub, dating from 1898, stands at the ancient St Thomas a Watering where a stream ran across the road on the line of Albany Street. Chaucer writes of this spot 'And forth we rode a little more than pace/Unto the watering of St Thomas./And there our Host began his horse arrest...' In *The Canterbury Tales* it is here outside what is now Tesco that the pilgrims draw lots to decide who will tell the first tale. More recently the pub has been associated with boxers including Henry Cooper who trained in the first-floor gym. The pub sign is a reproduction of the image of Becket made from 13th-century glass in Canterbury Cathedral.

Take the second exit on the left into Old Kent Road by crossing Tower Bridge Road (left) and passing the nursing home (which replaced the Bricklayers Arms) on the corner. On entering Old Kent Road there is the end of the flyover (right).

Continue down the main road and soon there is a lonely Regency house (left). On the right is Surrey Square.

Pass the Dun Cow Surgery (left) at the junction with Dunton Road where there was a toll gate. Continue past Tesco (left) to the crossroads where there is the Thomas a Becket pub (right; **2**).

Still keep forward and after just over half a mile (0.8km) there is the old North Peckham Civic Centre (right) which features a huge exterior mural.

The former **North Peckham Civic Centre**, now the Everlasting Arms church, was completed in 1967 when the ceramic mosaic mural by Adam Kossowski was added at the front. It dramatically recalls the Old Kent Road's history with images of the Romans, pilgrims, Henry V and Charles II. The artist also produced work for Aylesford Priory (see Stage 11) as part of his thanks to God for release from a Soviet labour camp.

The Pilgrims' Way

Adam Kossowski's mural in Old Kent Road

Later, on the corner of Commercial Way (right), is the former Kentish Drovers pub (**3**).

The **Kentish Drovers & Halfway House** dates from about 1840 and is famous for having England's longest pub sign: a curving painting depicting people on a rural Old Kent Road. The River Peck ran across the main road on the west side on its way from Peckham to the Thames. Drovers brought cattle up from Kent to Smithfield Market and for them the pub was about halfway between Deptford Bridge and Southwark.

On the right is Goldsmiths University of London.

Keep ahead, now best walking on the left-hand pavement, to go under a railway and join a one-way system. Turn left into New Cross Road. The road crosses railway lines at New Cross Gate and New Cross stations. ◄ Pass Deptford Street (left).

Keep ahead over Deptford Bridge crossing the Ravensbourne River, although the place is now best

STAGE 1A – SOUTHWARK TO SHOOTERS HILL

known for the railway bridge with Deptford Bridge station (**4**) spanning the road. Still keep forward at a junction to begin a long climb up Blackheath Hill to eventually emerge on the vast green open space of Blackheath (**5**).

BLACKHEATH

Here Wat Tyler gathered the Peasants Revolt in 1381, and Jack Cade in 1450 led a rebellion of men from Kent and Sussex to win reforms from Henry VI. Along the north side is the wall of Greenwich Park which formed the grounds of Henry VIII's Palace of Placentia. The King came to the gates here in January 1540 for his first official meeting with his fourth wife Anne of Cleves who had come down the road from Shooters Hill. All Saints church, built in 1853, is near the village. The Paragon, on the south-east side, is a residential Georgian masterpiece development by Richard Searles.

For Blackheath station
Go right to follow Goffers Road which runs across the heath to become Tranquil Vale and leads directly to the station (½ mile/0.8km).

Stay on Shooters Hill Road with, at first, grass on both sides. Walk on the left side and at the junction with Rochester Way use the underpass. After crossing the bridge bear left to emerge by the Sun in the Sands pub (left; **6**).

173

The Pilgrims' Way

Shortly, the main road is joined by the Old Dover Road (left). Continue on Shooters Hill Road to pass Woolwich Common (left). After a crossroads, at the junction for Eltham, go ahead up Shooters Hill.

> The **Sun in the Sands** pub dates from 1745 and its name is said to come from the sight of the setting sun seen through dust kicked up by sheep being herded into London. Travellers calling here include Georgian essayist William Hazlitt.

SHOOTERS HILL

The magnificent panorama of London on a clear day was once the first view of the capital for foreign visitors travelling from Dover. For pilgrims this was the last view of London. Samuel Pepys mentions the hill in his 1661 diary. The mounting block on the summit indicates the original site of the 1749 Bull Tavern which was much larger than the present 1881 pub. As a child at the end of the 18th century, Princess Charlotte was lodged on the hill for her education while her mother Princess Caroline lived at Blackheath. In the woods behind the church is Severndroog Castle, a tower built in 1784. But the landmark seen from central London is the 531-foot-high (162m) water tower erected in 1910. Woodlands Farm is the former Royal Arsenal Co-operative Society farm.

Look back here to see the view.

Just past Red Lion Place (left) is Gothic-style Prospect Cottage. This faces Christ Church where an 18th-century milestone shows 8 miles to London Bridge and 7 to Dartford. An added plate gives the number of miles to Ypres together with the number of casualties in the conflict. ◄

Continue up the hill, past a sign to Severndroog Castle (right), to reach the summit of the hill at The Bull.

For Woolwich Arsenal station
Bus 244 from Shrewsbury Lane by The Bull runs daily down to the station (1½ miles/2.4km).

STAGE 2A
Shooters Hill to Dartford

Start	The Bull, Shooters Hill
Finish	Dartford High Street
Distance	13 miles (21km)
Time	5½hrs
Maps	OS Explorer 162; Landranger 177
Refreshments	Pubs at Shooters Hill and Erith; cafe at Lesnes Abbey
Public transport	Railway stations at Woolwich Arsenal, Belvedere, Erith, Slade Green and Dartford; bus at Shooters Hill
Accommodation	Hotels at Woolwich Arsenal and Belvedere

From the great Shooters Hill viewpoint the road drops down to what was the start of Kent until the 20th century. The route then leaves the Roman road to head through ancient woodland to the attractive ruins of Lesnes Abbey which was dedicated to St Thomas Becket. Beyond further woodland, with occasional River Thames views, the path passes through Erith where pilgrims from East Anglia and the north crossed the river. A pier gives a seaside feel to the old port. Dartford is reached by way of a creek and ancient priory.

From Woolwich Arsenal station
Bus 244 to Shrewsbury Lane by The Bull runs daily (1½ miles/2.4km).

Continue past the pub, mounting block and **water tower** (left) to follow the road downhill to pass Woodlands Farm (left) and Thompsons Garden Centre. Stay on the main road to walk across the old Greater London–Kent border. The first building is the We-Anchor-in-Hope pub at Welling. Soon the modern Pilgrims' Way leaves the ancient Roman route by following the **Green Chain Walk** left into Wickham Street at Shoulder of Mutton Green.

THE PILGRIMS' WAY

Shoulder of Mutton Green takes its name from its peculiar shape. The owners, Queen's College, Oxford, tried to enclose the land in 1866 but the fences were torn down by locals and eventually the Metropolitan Board of Works made it a permanent public amenity. St Mary the Virgin church, built in 1955, has a wall painting by Hans Feibusch. The parish magazine is called *Pilgrims Way*.

Pass St Mary's church and after The Green Man the street becomes Chaucer Road. Go left down Keats Road to Poets Corner Community Garden. Bear right into Dryden Road.

At the far end go left into Glenmore Road and after only a few yards turn right, through a wide kissing gate, to **East Wickham** Open Space. Keep forward through the trees on a path which is soon boarded as it gently climbs. The way bears round to the left. At the top go right. On approaching buildings bear left across grass towards a seat. There is a metalled path running across the front of a bench. Go left to follow it to a viewpoint and down a slightly stepped way to a gate. Follow the road ahead to The Foresters Arms on the corner of Wickham Lane.

STAGE 2A – SHOOTERS HILL TO DARTFORD

Go left and then right up Cemetery Road. After the Plumstead Cemetery lodges (right) the road turns sharp left to follow the cemetery wall downhill. After Woodside Cottage (right) keep forward into the trees of **Bostall Woods**. At a path junction turn right. The way runs up and down through the trees. On the far side the path runs up a few steps to pass Bostall Heath Bowling Club. Cross the road and go to the right of the car park to walk over the open heath to a pedestrian crossing at Bostall Hill.

Cross the road and turn right. Ignore all turnings, including a Green Chain sign, to reach a crossroads. Go ahead over the end of Knee Hill and at once turn left along the Knee Hill pavement for a few yards. Turn right to rejoin the Green Chain by following a residential road

map continues on page 181

which bends left in front of flats to run down to Hurst Lane. Go right and at the next junction cross the road to enter **Lesnes Abbey Wood** at the kissing gate. The path is on high ground before running downhill. Go right to reach a pond (right). Where paths appear to be parallel take the left hand one. Cross New Road at kissing gates. Go over a cross path but at a second junction turn left. The valley path runs directly to the ruins of **Lesnes Abbey**.

LESNES ABBEY

Lesnes Abbey cloister

Lesnes Abbey was founded in 1178 by Richard de Lucy who had helped Henry II to secure the appointment of Becket as Archbishop of Canterbury. Lucy, although once excommunicated by Becket, dedicated the Augustinian abbey to the Virgin Mary and new saint Thomas Becket. The founder retired as chief justiciar, or government head, and joined his community here where he died in 1179. The small monastery was closed by Cardinal Thomas Wolsey in 1525. Much of the stone slowly disappeared, although the outline of the church, cloister, kitchen with hatch for serving dole and refectory survive.

Daffodils flower in profusion on the hill and bluebells in the wood every spring. The monks' garden has been restored. In summer the feast of Corpus Christi is celebrated with a procession in the church ruins. On the low ground to the north is Thamesmead which the monks knew as drained marshland pasture liable to flooding during extreme River Thames high tides.

Stage 2a – Shooters Hill to Dartford

Walk to the northern end of the abbey buildings, near the 400-year-old mulberry tree, and turn right (east) to follow a path uphill to a church window viewpoint where the London landmarks can be seen beyond the abbey.

Stay on this path but before it bears right into the woodland bear left, by a waymark, on a path that passes through a gap in the scrub and down steps. Turn left to reach a gate by the road. ▶ At once go right and right again into Leather Bottle Lane which is marked 'Byway 7' and runs along the bottom of the woodland. At the far end the lane rejoins the Green Chain. Pass Kingswood Avenue (left) to turn right into St Augustine's Road. The 400-year-old Ye Olde Leather Bottle was on the right until recently.

Take Upper Abbey Road opposite the inn site. At the Picardy Road junction bear left to the shop before crossing the road. (But keep forward for Belvedere station). Climb up the stepped pavement opposite the shop to follow Halt Robin Road.

Lesnes Abbey mulberry tree and London

A gateway leads to the bus stops on Abbey Road.

For Belvedere station
Walk down Picardy Road to Lower Road. Station Road is almost opposite (½ mile/0.8km).

Go over a crossroads and downhill to enter Frank's Park (right). Stay on the path just inside the woods. Halfway across the woodland there is suddenly an open valley with a playground.

At the far end keep ahead down Valley Road and left into Pembroke Road. At the bend go right to find a footbridge by the telephone box. The bridge crosses high above the railway and main road to reach Erith's ancient church.

ERITH

The Old Church has Lesnes Abbey tiles and tombstones in the vestry and tower. The monastery owned land on the Essex bank across the water where sheep were grazed and a ferry maintained. Canterbury-bound pilgrims from East Anglia boarded a ferry a little further north at Rainham village to land at Erith Causeway. The last ferry ran in 1954. The port of Erith was used by Henry VIII to fit out naval ships and in the early 19th century it had the air of a seaside resort as day trippers arrived by steamer from London. By the 20th century the major employer was Callender's Cables whose contracts included laying a pipeline under the English Channel. Today's pier with free admission brings a return to the feel of a resort.

Pass the church lychgate (left), cross the road and turn left to find Corinthian Manor Way leading to the Thames riverside. Turn right, downstream, but where the promenade divides take the lower path. Eventually the path turns inland at the former Police Station where a plaque marks the pilgrim ferry point. Go left up the High Street to Erith Playhouse.

For Erith station
Where the riverside path joins the High Street go right, then left into Walnut Tree Road and after a few yards right into Stonewood Road which leads under the main road to the station (¼ mile/0.4km).

STAGE 2A – SHOOTERS HILL TO DARTFORD

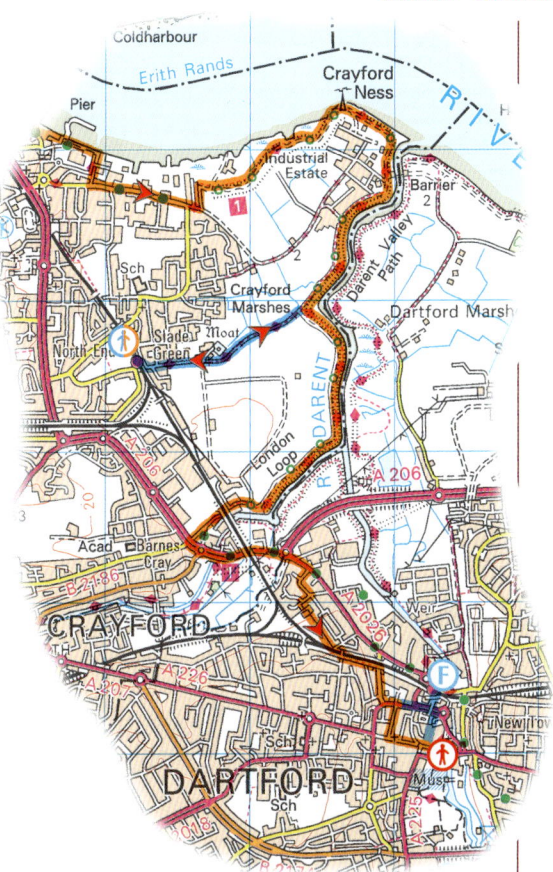

Go down the passage between the former Cross Keys and the theatre to find steps leading to a promenade. Follow this wide riverside walk past Erith Deep Water Wharf pier. Morrisons store is to the right. Where the promenade suddenly ends and the way turns inland keep forward on the road. At a junction with Wheatley Terrace bear half left to go up Appold Street to a main road.

The Pilgrims' Way

Later Dartford's high level bridge can be seen.

Turn left to walk along Manor Road which has many small buildings and scrap yards. ◄ Soon after a main junction turn left down a lane at the Erith Yacht Club sign. After a sharp bend the way rises. Keep to the right side of the lane. At the second bend keep ahead on a causeway running ahead across Erith Saltings to the Thames.

Crayford Ness, the most northerly point, is marked by a signpost and low concrete walls below a radar station monitoring shipping for the Thames Barrier. Continue to the confluence with the **River Darent**. There is no bridge, only a flood barrier, so the riverside path turns up Dartford Creek which is the modern London boundary with Kent. Pass through squeeze stiles by gates each side of the barrier service road. But where the path divides go ahead only to reach Slade Green station. The main route continues with the left fork. Here the way suddenly has a hedge and fencing to the right as it runs along **Crayford Marshes**.

Dartford Priory's Manor Gatehouse

STAGE 2A – SHOOTERS HILL TO DARTFORD

For Slade Green station
From beyond the Darent flood barrier follow the right fork which becomes Moat Lane leading to the station (½ mile/0.8km).

Later the way leaves the Darent to follow the River Cray. ▶ Soon the path meets a massive recycling facility and turns sharp right. Follow the enclosed path which becomes a pavement as it joins a road. ▶ Pass under the London-Dartford railway line. Keep ahead to a main road at the Jolly Farmers Roundabout (left) at **Barnes Cray**. At once cross the road at the pedestrian lights. Go left to cross the end of Crayford Way and continue east along Thames Road which crosses the River Cray. Go under the railway ahead and continue up the main road past a roundabout.

Go right down Burnham Crescent. This suburban road bears left to a crossroads. Turn right and after a very short distance go left along a wide footpath known as Willow Walk. Soon the way opens out by a playground and grass. The path runs gently uphill to pass the end of a road (left) and become enclosed. Here the now narrow path takes a double bend to cross high above the railway. After joining a lane take the left fork. Here a partly stepped path runs downhill to Priory Road South. Opposite is the wall of Dartford Priory.

> **Dartford Priory**, England's only Dominican convent, was founded in 1346. After dissolution in 1539 the site was replaced by a manor house where Anne of Cleves lived following her divorce from Henry VIII. Elizabeth I stayed twice. The mansion's gatehouse survives as a wedding venue.

Turn right along the road to pass an ancient doorway in the priory wall (left) and the Manor Gatehouse. At the junction go left past Pizza Hut. Only to reach Dartford station keep forward across the junction to find the entrance below the footbridge ahead.

Here there is a handy seat made from railway sleepers.

Beware lorries leaving gateways on the left.

For the ancient centre of Dartford go right down Kent Street by crossing at the pedestrian lights and passing Leverton's (left). At the far end turn left to join the original main road. Continue up the High Street, past the Methodist Church (left) and the Royal Victoria & Bull (right).

DARTFORD

Dartford means 'Darent ford'. Holy Trinity church was built about 1080 by Bishop Gundulf and enlarged during the reign of Henry III when his sister Isabella was married there by proxy to Holy Roman Emperor Frederick II. In 1415 Henry V gave thanks at the church on his return from the Battle of Agincourt when the wall painting of St George may already have been completed. The choir room was a chapel dedicated to Becket.

Pilgrims often stayed in the High Street at The Bull's Head (now Bull's Head Yard), Le Bell (now One Bell Corner) or The Bull with a galleried yard which survives as the Royal Victoria & Bull. This was an overnight stop for Jane Austen and the prefix follows a visit by Queen Victoria in her accession year, 1837. The milestone outside records 15 miles from London. The Wat Tyler pub is named after the Peasants' Revolt leader who drank there on Whit Friday 1381 on his way from Canterbury to Blackheath. Entry to the church is via its cafe and is open Monday to Saturday, 9am to 3pm.

For Dartford station
From the High Street go through The Bull's Head Yard entrance almost opposite WH Smith to join Suffolk Road and keep forward to cross the footbridge to the station (¼ mile/0.4km).

STAGE 3A
Dartford to Otford

Start	Dartford High Street
Finish	Otford pond
Distance	11½ miles (18.5km)
Time	5hrs
Maps	OS Explorer 162 and 147; Landranger 177 and 188
Refreshments	Pubs at Dartford, Darenth, Horton Kirby, Farningham, Eynsford and Shoreham; tea shops at Lullingstone and Shoreham
Public transport	Railway stations at Dartford, Farningham Road, Eynsford, Shoreham and Otford
Accommodation	Dartford and Eynsford

Here the path is beside the River Darent, along the Darent Valley, and through villages of historic resonance long known to travellers making for Canterbury. 'And the still Darent, in whose waters cleane/Ten thousand fishes play...' wrote the poet Edmund Spenser in 1586 while Samuel Palmer in the 1820s called Shoreham village 'the veil of heaven'. Historian Arthur Mee lived in the Darent Valley where he described the view from his house as 'a straight mile probably unique on the map of rural England, beginning with the site of a Roman house, passing a Norman castle, and ending at the site of a Saxon settlement; then if we lengthen our mile a little, heading on to a Tudor gateway in Lullingstone Park. Roman, Norman, Saxon, Tudor – it is all in line, and in sight from Eynsford Hill'.

From Dartford station

Go ahead from the station over Hanau Bridge to keep forward and join Suffolk Road leading to Bulls Head Yard and the High Street (¼ mile/0.4km).

Walk south from the High Street down Market Place. Keep forward to pass the library (left) and enter the park. At the bandstand bear half left on the grass and then

THE PILGRIMS' WAY

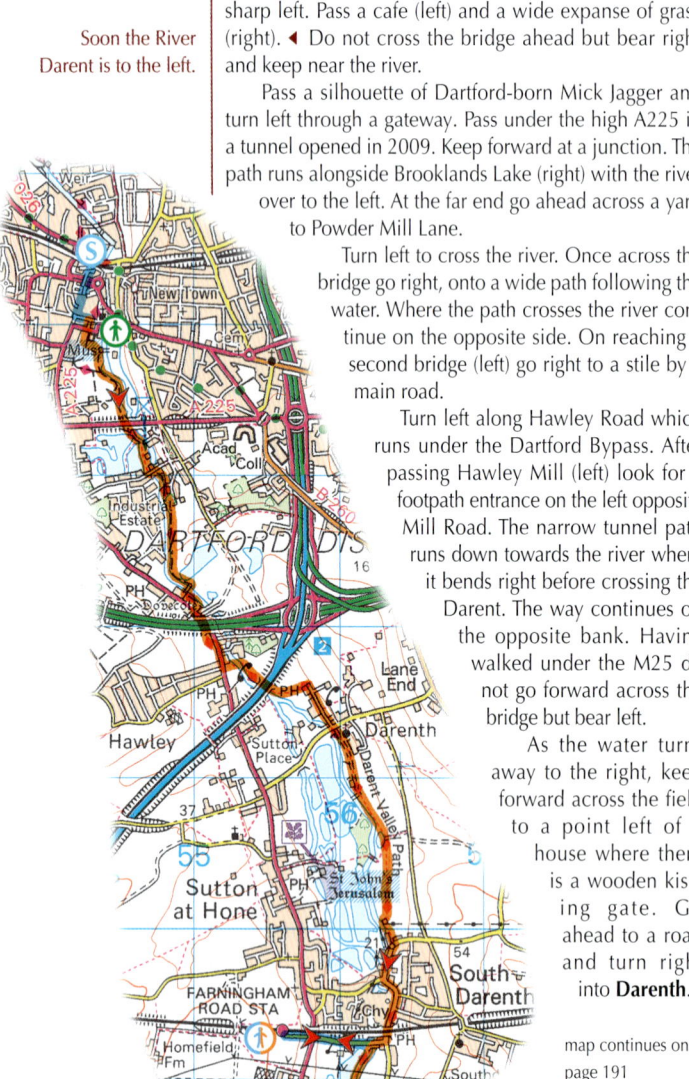

Soon the River Darent is to the left.

sharp left. Pass a cafe (left) and a wide expanse of grass (right). ◀ Do not cross the bridge ahead but bear right and keep near the river.

Pass a silhouette of Dartford-born Mick Jagger and turn left through a gateway. Pass under the high A225 in a tunnel opened in 2009. Keep forward at a junction. The path runs alongside Brooklands Lake (right) with the river over to the left. At the far end go ahead across a yard to Powder Mill Lane.

Turn left to cross the river. Once across the bridge go right, onto a wide path following the water. Where the path crosses the river continue on the opposite side. On reaching a second bridge (left) go right to a stile by a main road.

Turn left along Hawley Road which runs under the Dartford Bypass. After passing Hawley Mill (left) look for a footpath entrance on the left opposite Mill Road. The narrow tunnel path runs down towards the river where it bends right before crossing the Darent. The way continues on the opposite bank. Having walked under the M25 do not go forward across the bridge but bear left.

As the water turns away to the right, keep forward across the field to a point left of a house where there is a wooden kissing gate. Go ahead to a road and turn right into **Darenth**.

map continues on page 191

Stage 3a – Dartford to Otford

DARENTH

Darenth church, which includes Roman bricks, dates from the Saxon period and has a Norman sanctuary and chancel. Holes in the porch door are said to have come from shots fired by Oliver Cromwell's troops chasing Cavaliers down the valley. In 1195 Darenth manor, held by Canterbury Cathedral, was given to Rochester Cathedral in exchange for its land at Lambeth once secured by Bishop Gundulf. This is now the Archbishop of Canterbury's London home, Lambeth Palace. The Chequers Inn is partly Elizabethan.

Pass Vicarage Cottage (right) and soon there is The Chequers. Keep ahead to a junction at Parsonage Lane. Only go left uphill to visit the church. Cross the road to go forward on a very narrow path between the wide entrance to a fruit distribution depot (left) and a gateway (right). Later the enclosed route goes up steps and soon emerges by a field (left). Keep forward and where there is a fork bear right from the field into woodland to follow the river and pass a **lake**.

South Darenth

On emerging at a huge field go ahead in the direction of the **landmark chimney in South Darenth**. On the far side the way is enclosed before joining a drive and reaching, beyond a gate, a road in South Darenth.

> The chimney in **South Darenth** was built in 1881 for a paper mill which closed in 2003. The 10-arch railway viaduct was completed in 1860 for the London, Chatham and Dover railway running out of London's Blackfriars. Both Blackfriars and Darenth bridges were designed by Joseph Cubitt.

Turn right along Holmesdale Road. Ignore a turning across the river (right) and stay on the road round the bend. At the Jolly Miller and East Hill (left) keep forward up Horton Road. At the viaduct use the pavement on the left to go under the railway. Pass The Bridges pub and at once turn right into Station Road.

For Farningham Road station
After crossing the river in Station Road keep ahead. At a junction go forward uphill to the station (½ mile/0.8km).

Having crossed the river, turn left onto a footpath by the water. The path follows the River Darent (left) soon passing a ford and a footbridge. To avoid a garden spanning both river banks, the wooded path later veers away from the water to reach a playing field. Keep forward and pass a fenced grassy riverside area (left) and a cricket pavilion (right). A bridge leads across the river into **Horton Kirby** by a former mill site.

Continue past the village. Beyond the cricket ground car park, the path is ahead over grass to a kissing gate. Soon after another narrow gateway the path rejoins the river. Keep on the riverside path, which soon rises above the river in the woodland to Franks Lane Bridge.

Turn left over the bridge and keep forward along Franks Lane. On reaching houses go right, through a kissing gate. Follow the enclosed way with a cricket ground to the left. To the right there is a brief view of **Franks Hall**,

STAGE 3A – DARTFORD TO OTFORD

HORTON KIRBY

This was just Horton until 1691 when the last descendant of the Norman family once holding the castle married a 'Kirkby'. The castle, built for Bishop Odo of Bayeux who arrived in England in 1066 with his half-brother William the Conqueror, is now Court Lodge Farm with a dovecot visible from the churchyard's back gate. The church was built about 1190 when masons came from Canterbury. The tower is 19th century. The Fighting Cocks, at the south end of the village, has a garden leading down to the river. New housing by the river replaces Westminster Mill, originally a corn mill producing paper and which closed in 1991.

an Elizabethan mansion. At the far end, after a sharp double bend, the path rejoins the river (right). Stay by the water as it bends again twice to go under the M20 and shortly afterwards the A20. Cross the footbridge and keep

Franks Hall

FARNINGHAM

The cattle screen in the river, to stop stock from wandering, was built around 1750 before the bridge replaced a ford. An early lord of the manor was St Alphege, Archbishop of Canterbury. A successor was Wadard who is depicted in the Bayeux Tapestry and features on the village sign. Another holder of the manor was St Thomas More's grandson Antony Roper, whose 1597 bequest still benefits the parish. His monument is in the church (north wall of chancel). The Manor House was the last home of William Bligh of the *Bounty*. Sir Henry Irving's godson Irving Albery lived there from 1921 to 1965. Both The Lion and The Pied Bull, on different sides of the river, are former coaching inns on the London to Dover route.

Cattle screen at Farningham

Ahead is a fine corn mill.

on the opposite bank's high path to reach **Farningham** by the Lion Hotel. ◀

Turn right past The Lion to follow the High Street. Go left into Sparepenny Lane. After 200 yards go left down steps to a kissing gate. Follow a path parallel to the lane (right). After fields, and a wood, go up steps to a kissing gate at Furlongs Farm. Rejoin the lane for Eynsford.

Stage 3a – Dartford to Otford

The appointment in 1163 of a new parish priest to **Eynsford** by Thomas Becket against the wishes of patron and royal tenant William de Eynsford was the beginning of the breakdown in relations between king and archbishop. Becket excommunicated the patron and only after a blazing quarrel between king and primate did the archbishop back down. The ruined early Norman castle, home of William de Eynsford, is open daily.

For Eynsford station
At the bottom of Sparepenny Lane go left through the village and over the river to the church. Turn right for the station (¾ mile/1.2km).

Only for the village centre and ford go left. The walk continues to the right,

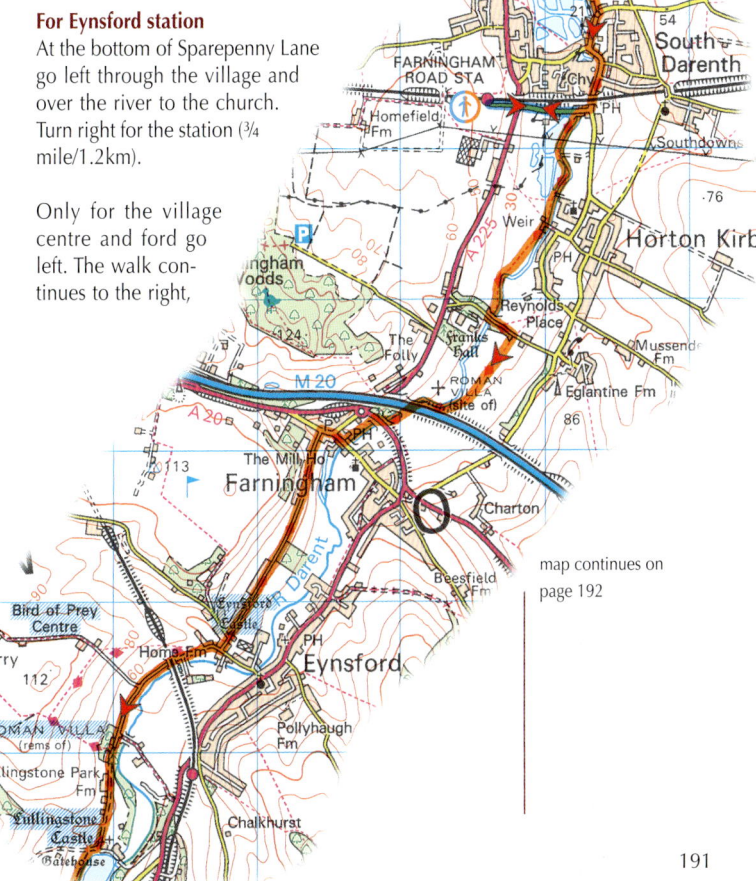

map continues on page 192

along the road. Darenth Cottage is on the right. The road passes under the railway viaduct and in less than a mile reaches **Lullingstone Roman Villa** (right).

Lullingstone Roman Villa dates from AD80. Towards the end of the 4th century, 200 years before St Augustine landed in Kent, the family embraced Christianity and turned a room into a chapel. The villa is open daily with refreshments available.

Do not cross the river but keep forward by the English Heritage building (right). The lane beyond the Roman villa leads to **Lullingstone Castle**.

Lullingstone Castle was home of Henry VIII's jousting champion Sir John Peche and is now occupied by his descendants, the Hart Dyke family. Henry visited on his way to Otford and later Queen Anne stayed. The rules of lawn tennis were devised on the lawn by Sir William Hart Dyke in 1873. This century, plant hunter Tom Hart Dyke has created a World Garden of Plants in the grounds. The little church of St Botolph is known as the 'church on the lawn' and can be visited by passing pilgrims via the gatehouse.

Walk to the right side of the gates at the end of the road to find a kissing gate. Beyond here a wooded path runs alongside the river (left) to Kingfisher Bridge. To the right there is the **Lullingstone Park** Visitor Centre and cafe.

Ford at Eynsford

Go ahead through a wooden kissing gate to a wide path running alongside the road (left). Soon there are the **Castle Farm** buildings (left) bisected by the river.

The Alexander family has been farming at **Castle Farm** since arriving from Scotland by train in 1892 with 17 Ayrshire dairy cows. The farm is now best known for its huge lavender fields planted only in 2000. There is also a small Norfolk Royals apple orchard and one remaining hop field. The Hop Shop sells farm produce.

At the far end go down steps and cross the road with care. Go through a gap by a gate to follow the top of a bank by the hop field (left). At the end go through a gate in a line of trees and across a sloping field, go over a concrete cross path and forward as the path bears half left across a field which gently rises to the centre. In the far corner of the field go through a gate. ▶ Later there is a wire fence (right). At the end of the field go through a wooden kissing gate to follow a narrow path by the river.

There is a glimpse of the river (left).

On reaching a metalled lane turn left towards the mill entrance but at once go right, along a short path which crosses the river. Turn right, along the riverside path to follow the water (right). The path leads past Water House, where the artist Samuel Palmer lived, into the centre of **Shoreham**.

SHOREHAM

Shoreham means 'home in the cleft'. The church contains the Westminster Abbey pulpit used at Queen Victoria's coronation. In the south wall there is a Burne-Jones window commemorating geologist Sir John Prestwich. Buried in the churchyard is villager and bible illustrator Harold Copping who produced the best seller *Copping Bible* in 1911. Artist Samuel Palmer was steeped in the Bible when he came in 1826 and compared the countryside to Psalm 65 with 'folds full of sheep' and 'valleys...thick with corn'. He roamed the footpaths at night and that year produced *Early Morning* showing a rabbit on a footpath. In 1926 Eric Ravilious was so inspired by an exhibition of Palmer's work that he walked 20 miles with fellow landscape artist Paul Nash to see the Shoreham countryside for himself. Palmer's painting of the church called *Coming from Church Evensong, Shoreham* is in the Tate collection. Inside the church is Royal Academician Charles Cope's 1875 painting depicting the vicar's son returning to the church having commanded an expedition searching for David Livingstone. A large cross carved into the hill commemorates World War I dead.

Go left along the road, not over the bridge, to pass Palmer's earlier home, Ivy Cottage (left). At a sharp bend it is possible to go ahead through the lychgate and up the brick path which passes the church. Go through the kissing gate and turn right to return to the road opposite Shoreham Place.

For Shoreham station
After leaving the churchyard to return to the road go left to the railway bridge (300 yards/0.2km)

Turn left up the road but well before reaching Shoreham station go right, on a footpath, which runs between wooden posts and along a thin belt of trees. Keep ahead on this mainly fenced path which crosses a golf course and reaches a kissing gate at a cricket field. The path goes ahead, within the game's boundary, to pass the cricket pavilion (right).

The fenced path soon crosses a metalled lane where the Darent Valley Walk turns right. But the PW continues forward. ▶ The path begins to run downhill and then widens when joined by another from the right. The track becomes metalled to reach Otford High Street opposite Otford Tearooms.

Turn left for the village centre at the pond.

Soon Otford church can be seen ahead.

For Otford station

From the pond at the end of the High Street walk along Station Road and bear right before the railway bridge (¼ mile/0.4km).

The route to Canterbury continues with Stage 9.

Romero Way: Roman Catholic St George's Cathedral Southwark to Anglican Southwark Cathedral. 1 mile (1.6km)

Leave St George's Cathedral by turning right to circle the site. At St George's Circus keep ahead into Borough Road. Go left into Lancaster Street and right along King James Street. At the end go left and right into Webber Street. At Great Suffolk Street bear right to the crossroads and turn left up Southwark Bridge Road. Pass the Welsh Chapel (left).

At the Union Street traffic lights go right into Flat Iron Square and left into O'Meara Street to pass the Church of the Precious Blood (right). At the far end use the crossing (left) to go right along Southwark Street and left into Redcross Way. At the T-junction turn right to follow Park Street. After the bend Southwark Cathedral's tower can be seen ahead above Borough Market.

THE PILGRIMS' WAY

APPENDIX A
Itinerary planner

Stage	Start/finish	Distance	Cumulative distance	Station at start	Station on route	Station at end	Accommodation	Refreshments	Page
1	Winchester–Alresford	9 miles (14.4km)	9 miles (14.4km)	Winchester		(Bus to Winchester)	Winchester, Alresford,	Kings Worthy, Itchen Abbas, Alresford	28
2	Alresford–Alton	12 miles (19.3km)	21 miles (33.7km)			Alton	Alresford, Four Marks, Alton	Four Marks, Chawton, Alton	38
3	Alton–Farnham	11 miles (17.7km)	32 miles (51.4km)	Alton		Farnham	Alton, Farnham	Lower Froyle, Bentley, Farnham	47
4	Farnham–Guildford	10½ miles (16.8km)	42½ miles (68.3km)	Farnham		Guildford	Farnham, Puttenham, Guildford	Puttenham, Compton, St Catherine's, Guildford	57
5	Guildford–Box Hill	13½ miles (21.7km)	56 miles (90.1km)	Guildford	Gomshall	Box Hill & Westhumble	Guildford, Shere, Westhumble	Shere, Gomshall, Abinger Hammer, Denbies, Westhumble	66
6	Box Hill–Merstham	9¾ miles (15.6km)	65¾ miles (105.8km)	Box Hill & Westhumble	Betchworth, Reigate	Merstham	Westhumble, Betchworth, Reigate Hill	Reigate Hill, Merstham	78
7	Merstham–Oxted	8 miles (12.8km)	73¾ miles (118.6km)	Merstham		Oxted	Oxted	Whitehill, Oxted	87

Appendix A – Itinerary planner

Stage	Start/finish	Distance	Cumulative distance	Station at start	Station on route	Station at end	Accommodation	Refreshments	Page
8	Oxted–Otford	12 miles (19.3km)	85¾ miles (138km)	Oxted	Westerham Hill (bus 246 to Bromley South station)	Otford	Dunton Green	Dunton Green, Otford	95
9	Otford–Wrotham	5¾ miles (9.2km)	91 miles (146.4km) From London 38¾ miles (62.3km)	Otford		Borough Green & Wrotham	Wrotham	Kemsing, Wrotham	103
10	Wrotham–Halling	7¼ miles (11.6km)	98¾ miles (158.9km) 46 miles (73.9km)	Borough Green & Wrotham		Halling	Wrotham	Halling	108
11	Halling–Aylesford	4¾ miles (7.6km)	103½ miles (166.5km) 50¾ miles (81.5km)	Halling		Aylesford	Aylesford Priory, Aylesford	Aylesford Priory, Aylesford	115
11a	Peters Village–Rochester	4½ miles (7.2km)				Rochester	Rochester	Wouldham, Rochester	122
12	Aylesford–Harrietsham	11 miles (17.7km)	114½ miles (184.2km) 61¾ miles (99.2km)	Aylesford	Thurnham (Bearsted station), Hollingbourne	Harrietsham	Aylesford, Thurnham	Boxley, Detling, Thurnham, Hollingbourne, Harrietsham	129

THE PILGRIMS' WAY

Stage	Start/finish	Distance	Cumulative distance	Station at start	Station on route	Station at end	Accommodation	Refreshments	Page
13	Harrietsham–Boughton Lees	11 miles (17.7km)	125½ miles (201.9km) 72¾ miles (116.9km)	Harrietsham	Lenham, Charing	Boughton Lees (Wye station)	Lenham, Boughton Lees	Lenham, Charing, Boughton Lees	139
14	Boughton Lees–Chilham	6 miles (9.6km)	131½ miles (211.6km) 78¾ miles (126.5km)	Boughton Lees (Wye station)		Chilham	Boughton Lees, Chilham	Chilham	149
15	Chilham–Canterbury	7 miles (11.2km)	138½ miles (222.8km) 85¾ miles (138km)	Chilham		Canterbury West	Chilham, Canterbury	Old Wives Lees, Harbledown, Canterbury	156
From London									
1a	Southwark–Shooters Hill	8½ miles (13.6km)		London Bridge	New Cross, New Cross Gate, Deptford, Blackheath	Woolwich Arsenal	Southwark, Deptford Bridge, Woolwich Arsenal	Southwark, Blackheath, Shooters Hill	166
2a	Shooters Hill–Dartford	13 miles (21km)	21½ miles (34.6km)	Woolwich Arsenal	Belvedere, Erith, Slade Green	Dartford	Woolwich Arsenal, Belvedere, Dartford	Lesnes Abbey, Erith, Dartford	175
3a	Dartford–Otford	11½ miles (18.5km)	33 miles (53.1km)	Dartford	Farningham Road, Eynsford, Shoreham	Otford	Dartford, Eynsford	Darenth, Horton Kirby, Farningham, Eynsford, Lullingstone, Shoreham	185

198

APPENDIX B

Accommodation

From Winchester to Canterbury

Winchester
Cathedral Cottage
19 Colebrook Street
SO23 9LH
tel 01962 878975
www.cathedralcottagebandb.co.uk

Alresford
Applewood
2 Orchard Close
SO24 9PY
tel 01962 732332
Near PW

Four marks
Travelodge
156 Winchester Road
GU34 5HZ
tel 08719 846002
www.travelodge.co.uk

Alton
The Swan
High Street
GU34 1AT
tel 01420 83777
www.oldenglishinns.co.uk
On PW

Puttenham
Puttenham Eco Camping Barn
GU3 1AR
tel 01483 811001
www.puttenhambarn.uk
On PW

Guildford
Travelodge
Woodbridge Meadows
GU1 1BD
tel 08719 846295
www.travelodge.co.uk

The Angel Hotel
91 High St
GU1 3DP
tel 01483 564555
www.angelpostinghouse.com

Shere
Rookery Nook
The Square
GU5 9HG
tel 01483 209382
www.rookerynook.info
On PW

Westhumble
Denbies Vineyard Hotel
Bradley Lane
RH5 6AA
tel 01306 876777
www.denbies.co.uk
On PW

Mercure Burford Bridge Hotel
RH5 6BX
tel 020 7660 0684
www.accorhotels.com
At foot of Box Hill, north of foot tunnel

The Pilgrims' Way

Betchworth
The Red Lion
Old Road
RH3 7DS
tel 01737 843336
www.theredlionbetchworth.com
¾ mile (1.2km) pavement walk south from station

Reigate Hill
Bridge House Hotel
RH2 9RP
www.oyorooms.com/gb
Approach having crossed footbridge

Oxted
Meads Bed & Breakfast
23 Granville Road
RH8 0BX
tel 01883 730115
www.bandbmeads.co.uk

Dunton Green
Donnington Manor Hotel
London Rd
TN13 2TD
tel 01732 462681
www.bw-donningtonmanor.co.uk
On PW between Chevening and Otford

Wrotham
The Bull
Bull Lane
TN15 7RF
tel 01732 789800
www.thebullhotel.com

Aylesford
The Priory
ME20 7BX
tel 01622 717272
www.thefriars.org.uk
On PW

Thurnham
Black Horse Inn
Pilgrims Way
ME14 3LE
tel 01622 737185
www.blackhorsekent.co.uk

Lenham
The Dog & Bear Hotel
The Square
ME17 2PG
tel 01622 858219
www.dogandbearlenham.co.uk

The Flying Horse
TN25 4HH
tel 01233 620914
https://theflying.horse
On PW

Chilham
The Woolpack
The Street
CT4 8DL
tel 01227 730351
www.woolpackchilham.co.uk

Canterbury
Canterbury Lodge
63 London Rd
CT2 8JZ
tel 01227 768767
www.canterburylodge.uk
On PW

Canterbury Cathedral Lodge
tel 01227 865350
www.canterburycathedrallodge.org

YHA Canterbury
New Dover Road
CT1 3DT
tel 0345 371 9010
www.yha.org.uk

APPENDIX B – ACCOMMODATION

From London to Otford

London Southwark
Premier Inn
Spur Inn Yard
135 Borough High Street
SE1 1NP
tel 0333 234 6478
www.premierinn.com

Dover Castle Hostel
6A Great Dover Street
Borough
SE1 4XW
tel 020 7403 7773
www.dovercastlehostel.com
Close to Southwark Cathedral start

Deptford Bridge
Travelodge
Blackheath Road
SE10 8DA
tel 0871 984 6508
www.travelodge.co.uk
On PW

Premier Inn Greenwich
43 Greenwich High Road
SE10 8LS
tel 0333 321 9206
www.premierinn.com
On PW

Blackheath
The Clarendon Hotel
Montpelier Row
SE3 0RW
tel 020 8318 4321
www.clarendonhotel.com
Near church

Woolwich Travelodge
129 Powis Street
Woolwich
SE18 6JL
tel 0871 984 6510
www.travelodge.co.uk

Belvedere
Belvedere Travelodge
Clydesdale Way
Picardy Manorway
DA17 6FP
tel 0871 559 1882
www.travelodge.co.uk
North of Belvedere Station

Dartford
The Royal Victoria And Bull Hotel
1 High Street
DA1 1DU
tel 01322 224415
On PW

Eynsford
The Castle Hotel
High Street
DA4 0AB
tel 01322 633917
www.castlehotelkent.com
Opposite Eynsford Castle

Rochester diversion

Rochester
Royal Victoria & Bull
16-18 High St ME1 1PX
tel 01634 819245
www.rvbhotel.com

APPENDIX C
Further information

Useful websites
www.canterbury-cathedral.org
Canterbury Cathedral has dedicated Pilgrim pages.

www.thepilgrimsway.co.uk
A blog by Cicerone guide author Leigh Hatts.

www.britishpilgrimage.org
British Pilgrmage Trust

Transport
South Western Railway
(Winchester, Alton, Farnham and Guildford)
www.southwesternrailway.com

Southern Railway
(Box Hill & Westhumble, Reigate, Merstham, Caterham and Oxted)
www.southernrailway.com

Southeastern
(London Bridge, New Cross, Deptford, Blackheath, Woolwich Arsenal, Abbey Wood, Erith, Slade Green, Dartford, Farningham Road, Eynsford, Shoreham, Otford, Kemsing, Borough Green & Wrotham, Halling, Aylesford, Bearsted, Hollingbourne, Harrietsham. Lenham, Charing, Wye, Chilham and Canterbury West.)
www.southeasternrailway.co.uk

Great Western Railway
(Gomshall and Betchworth)
www.gwr.com

Transport for London
www.tfl.gov.uk

Tourist Information Centres

Winchester
The Guildhall
Winchester
SO23 9GH
tel 01962 840500
www.visitwinchester.co.uk
Mon–Sat 10am–5pm
Sun 10am–3pm

Guildford
155 High St
Guildford
GU1 3AJ
tel 01483 444333
www.visitsurrey.com
Tue–Sat 10am–4.30pm

Canterbury
The Beaney House
18 High Street
Canterbury
CT1 2RA
tel 01227 862162
www.canterburymuseums.co.uk
Mon–Sat 10am–5pm
Sun 11am–4pm

APPENDIX D
Further reading

Albin (ed), Hugo O, *Thomas More and Canterbury*, Downside Abbey Books, 1994

Belloc, Hilaire, *The Old Road*, Nabu Press, 2010

du Boulay, Shirley, *The Road to Canterbury: A modern pilgrimage*, Harper Collins, 1994

Bright, Derek, *The Pilgrims' Way: Fact and Fiction of an Ancient Trackway*, The History Press, 2011

Cartwright, Julia, *The Pilgrims' Way from Winchester to Canterbury*, British Library, Historical Print Editions, 2011

Chaucer, Geoffrey, *The Canterbury Tales* (translated by David Wright), Oxford University Press, 2011

Duggan, Anne, *Thomas Becket*, Bloomsbury, 2004

Eliot, TS, *Murder in the Catherdral* Faber & Faber, 2001

Guy, John, *Thomas Becket: Warrior, Priest, Rebel, Victim: A 900-Year-Old Story Retold*, Penguin, 2013

Jennett, Sean, *The Pilgrims' Way: From Winchester to Canterbury*, Cassell, 1971

Pennell, Joseph, *A Canterbury Pilgrimage*, University of Alberta Press, 2015

Reynolds, Kev, *The North Downs Way*, Cicerone, 2017

Urry, William, *Thomas Becket: His Last Days*, Sutton Publishing, 1999

NOTES

LISTING OF CICERONE GUIDES

BRITISH ISLES CHALLENGES, COLLECTIONS AND ACTIVITIES
Great Walks on the England Coast Path
Map and Compass
The Big Rounds
The Book of the Bivvy
The Book of the Bothy
The Mountains of England and Wales:
  Vol 1 Wales
  Vol 2 England
The National Trails
Walking the End to End Trail

SHORT WALKS SERIES
Short Walks Hadrian's Wall
Short Walks in the Lake District: Keswick, Borrowdale and Buttermere
Short Walks in the Lake District: Windermere Ambleside and Grasmere
Short Walks in the Lake District: Coniston and Langdale
Short Walks in Arnside and Silverdale
Short Walks in Nidderdale
Short Walks in Northumberland: Wooler, Rothbury, Alnwick and the coast
Short Walks on the Malvern Hills
Short Walks in Cornwall: Falmouth and the Lizard
Short Walks in Cornwall: Land's End and Penzance
Short Walks in the South Downs: Brighton, Eastbourne and Arundel
Short Walks in the Surrey Hills
Short Walks Winchester
Short Walks in Pembrokeshire: Tenby and the south
Short Walks on the Isle of Mull
Short Walks on the Orkney Islands

SCOTLAND
Ben Nevis and Glen Coe
Cycling in the Hebrides
Cycling the North Coast 500
Great Mountain Days in Scotland
Mountain Biking in Southern and Central Scotland
Mountain Biking in West and North West Scotland
Not the West Highland Way Scotland
Scotland's Best Small Mountains
Scotland's Mountain Ridges
Scottish Wild Country Backpacking
Short Walks in Dumfries and Galloway
Skye's Cuillin Ridge Traverse
The Borders Abbeys Way
The Great Glen Way
The Great Glen Way Map Booklet
The Hebridean Way
The Hebrides
The Isle of Mull
The Isle of Skye
The Skye Trail
The Southern Upland Way
The West Highland Way
West Highland Way Map Booklet
Walking Ben Lawers, Rannoch and Atholl
Walking in the Cairngorms
Walking in the Pentland Hills
Walking in the Scottish Borders
Walking in the Southern Uplands
Walking in Torridon, Fisherfield, Fannichs and An Teallach
Walking Loch Lomond and the Trossachs
Walking on Arran
Walking on Harris and Lewis
Walking on Jura, Islay and Colonsay
Walking on Rum and the Small Isles
Walking on the Orkney and Shetland Isles
Walking on Uist and Barra
Walking the Cape Wrath Trail
Walking the Corbetts
  Vol 1 South of the Great Glen
  Vol 2 North of the Great Glen
Walking the Galloway Hills
Walking the John o' Groats Trail
Walking the Munros
  Vol 1 — Southern, Central and Western Highlands
  Vol 2 — Northern Highlands and the Cairngorms
Winter Climbs in the Cairngorms
Winter Climbs: Ben Nevis and Glen Coe

NORTHERN ENGLAND ROUTES
Cycling the Reivers Route
Cycling the Way of the Roses
Hadrian's Cycleway
Hadrian's Wall Path
Hadrian's Wall Path Map Booklet
Pennine Way Map Booklet
The Coast to Coast Cycle Route
The Coast to Coast Walk
The Coast to Coast Map Booklet
The Pennine Way
Walking the Dales Way
The Dales Way Map Booklet

LAKE DISTRICT
Bikepacking in the Lake District
Cycling in the Lake District
Great Mountain Days in the Lake District
Joss Naylor's Lakes, Meres and Waters of the Lake District
Lake District Winter Climbs
Lake District:
  High Level and Fell Walks
  Low Level and Lake Walks
Mountain Biking in the Lake District
Outdoor Adventures with Children — Lake District
Scrambles in the Lake District —
  North
  South
Trail and Fell Running in the Lake District
Walking The Cumbria Way
Walking the Lake District Fells —
  Borrowdale
  Buttermere
  Coniston
  Keswick
  Langdale
  Mardale and the Far East
  Patterdale
  Wasdale
Walking the Tour of the Lake District

NORTH—WEST ENGLAND AND THE ISLE OF MAN
Cycling the Pennine Bridleway
Isle of Man Coastal Path
The Lancashire Cycleway
The Lune Valley and Howgills
Walking in Cumbria's Eden Valley
Walking in Lancashire
Walking in the Forest of Bowland and Pendle
Walking on the Isle of Man
Walking on the West Pennine Moors
Walking the Ribble Way
Walks in Silverdale and Arnside

NORTH—EAST ENGLAND, YORKSHIRE DALES AND PENNINES
Cycling in the Yorkshire Dales
Great Mountain Days in the Pennines
Mountain Biking in the Yorkshire Dales
The Cleveland Way and the Yorkshire Wolds Way
The Cleveland Way Map Booklet
The North York Moors
Trail and Fell Running in the Yorkshire Dales
Walking in County Durham
Walking in Northumberland
Walking in the North Pennines
Walking in the Yorkshire Dales:
  North and East
  South and West
Walking St Cuthbert's Way
Walking St Oswald's Way and Northumberland Coast Path

DERBYSHIRE, PEAK DISTRICT AND MIDLANDS
Cycling in the Peak District
Dark Peak Walks
Scrambles in the Dark Peak
Walking in Derbyshire
Walking in the Peak District — White Peak East
Walking in the Peak District — White Peak West

WALES AND WELSH BORDERS
Cycle Touring in Wales
Cycling Lon Las Cymru
Great Mountain Days in Snowdonia
Hillwalking in Shropshire
Mountain Walking in Snowdonia
Offa's Dyke Path
Offa's Dyke Map Booklet
Scrambles in Snowdonia
Snowdonia: 30 Low-level and Easy Walks
— North
— South
The Cambrian Way
The Pembrokeshire Coast Path
Pembrokeshire Coast Path Map Booklet
The Snowdonia Way
The Wye Valley Walk
Walking Glyndwr's Way
Walking in Carmarthenshire
Walking in Pembrokeshire
Walking in the Brecon Beacons
Walking in the Forest of Dean
Walking in the Wye Valley
Walking on Gower
Walking the Severn Way
Walking the Shropshire Way
Walking the Wales Coast Path

SOUTHERN ENGLAND
20 Classic Sportive Rides in South East England
20 Classic Sportive Rides in South West England
Cycling in the Cotswolds
Mountain Biking on the North Downs
Mountain Biking on the South Downs
Suffolk Coast and Heath Walks
The Cotswold Way
The Cotswold Way Map Booklet
The Kennet and Avon Canal
The Lea Valley Walk
The North Downs Way
North Downs Way Map Booklet
The Peddars Way and Norfolk Coast Path
The Pilgrims' Way
The Ridgeway National Trail
The Ridgeway Map Booklet
The South Downs Way
The South Downs Way Map Booklet
The Thames Path
The Thames Path Map Booklet
The Two Moors Way

Two Moors Way Map Booklet
Walking Hampshire's Test Way
Walking in Cornwall
Walking in Essex
Walking in Kent
Walking in London
Walking in Norfolk
Walking in the Chilterns
Walking in the Cotswolds
Walking in the Isles of Scilly
Walking in the New Forest
Walking in the North Wessex Downs
Walking on Dartmoor
Walking on Guernsey
Walking on Jersey
Walking on the Isle of Wight
Walking the Dartmoor Way
Walking the Jurassic Coast
Walking the Sarsen Way
Walking the South West Coast Path
South West Coast Path Map Booklet
— Vol 1: Minehead to St Ives
— Vol 2: St Ives to Plymouth
— Vol 3: Plymouth to Poole
Walks in the South Downs National Park
Cycling Land's End to John o' Groats

ALPS CROSS—BORDER ROUTES
100 Hut Walks in the Alps
Alpine Ski Mountaineering Vol 1 — Western Alps
The Karnischer Hohenweg
The Tour of the Bernina
Trail Running — Chamonix and the Mont Blanc region
Trekking Chamonix to Zermatt
Trekking in the Alps
Trekking in the Silvretta and Ratikon Alps
Trekking Munich to Venice
Trekking the Tour du Mont Blanc
Tour du Mont Blanc Map Booklet
Walking in the Alps

FRANCE, BELGIUM, AND LUXEMBOURG
Camino de Santiago — Via Podiensis
Chamonix Mountain Adventures
Cycle Touring in France
Cycling London to Paris
Cycling the Canal de la Garonne
Cycling the Canal du Midi
Mont Blanc Walks
Mountain Adventures in the Maurienne
Short Treks on Corsica
The GR5 Trail
The GR5 Trail — Vosges and Jura Benelux and Lorraine
The Grand Traverse of the Massif Central
The Moselle Cycle Route
Trekking in the Vanoise

Trekking the Cathar Way
Trekking the GR10
Trekking the GR20 Corsica
Trekking the Robert Louis Stevenson Trail
Via Ferratas of the French Alps
Walking in Provence — East
Walking in Provence — West
Walking in the Auvergne
Walking in the Briançonnais
Walking in the Dordogne
Walking in the Haute Savoie: North
Walking in the Haute Savoie: South
Walking on Corsica
Walking the Brittany Coast Path
Walking in the Ardennes

PYRENEES AND FRANCE/SPAIN CROSS—BORDER ROUTES
Shorter Treks in the Pyrenees
The Pyrenean Haute Route
The Pyrenees
Trekking the Cami dels Bons Homes
Trekking the GR11 Trail
Walks and Climbs in the Pyrenees

SPAIN AND PORTUGAL
Camino de Santiago: Camino Frances
Costa Blanca Mountain Adventures
Cycling the Camino de Santiago
Mountain Walking in Mallorca
Mountain Walking in Southern Catalunya
Spain's Sendero Historico: The GR1
The Andalucian Coast to Coast Walk
The Camino del Norte and Camino Primitivo
The Camino Ingles and Ruta do Mar
The Mountains Around Nerja
The Sierras of Extremadura
Trekking in Mallorca
Trekking in the Canary Islands
Trekking the GR7 in Andalucia
Walking and Trekking in the Sierra Nevada
Walking in Andalucia
Walking in Catalunya — Barcelona Girona Pyrenees
Walking in the Picos de Europa
Walking La Via de la Plata and Camino Sanabres
Walking on Gran Canaria
Walking on La Gomera and El Hierro
Walking on La Palma
Walking on Lanzarote and Fuerteventura
Walking on Tenerife
Walking on the Costa Blanca
Walking the Camino dos Faros
Portugal's Rota Vicentina
The Camino Portugues
Walking in Portugal
Walking in the Algarve

Walking on Madeira
Walking on the Azores

SWITZERLAND
Switzerland's Jura Crest Trail
The Swiss Alps
Tour of the Jungfrau Region
Trekking the Swiss Via Alpina
Walking in Arolla and Zinal
Walking in the Bernese Oberland — Jungfrau region
Walking in the Engadine — Switzerland
Walking in the Valais
Walking in Ticino
Walking in Zermatt and Saas-Fee

GERMANY
Hiking and Cycling in the Black Forest
The Danube Cycleway Vol 1
The Rhine Cycle Route
The Westweg
Walking in the Bavarian Alps

POLAND, SLOVAKIA, ROMANIA, HUNGARY AND BULGARIA
The Danube Cycleway Vol 2
The High Tatras
The Mountains of Romania

SCANDINAVIA, ICELAND AND GREENLAND
Hiking in Norway — South
Trekking the Kungsleden
Trekking in Greenland — The Arctic Circle Trail
Walking and Trekking in Iceland

SLOVENIA, CROATIA, SERBIA, MONTENEGRO AND ALBANIA
Hiking Slovenia's Juliana Trail
Mountain Biking in Slovenia
The Islands of Croatia
The Julian Alps of Slovenia
The Mountains of Montenegro
The Peaks of the Balkans Trail
The Slovene Mountain Trail
Walking in Slovenia: The Karavanke
Walks and Treks in Croatia

ITALY
Alta Via 1 — Trekking in the Dolomites
Alta Via 2 — Trekking in the Dolomites
Day Walks in the Dolomites
Italy's Grande Traversata delle Alpi
Italy's Sibillini National Park
Ski Touring and Snowshoeing in the Dolomites
The Way of St Francis
Trekking Gran Paradiso: Alta Via 2
Trekking in the Apennines
Trekking the Giants' Trail: Alta Via 1 through the Italian Pennine Alps
Via Ferratas of the Italian Dolomites Vol 1
Vol 2
Walking in Abruzzo
Walking in Italy's Cinque Terre
Walking in Italy's Stelvio National Park
Walking in Sicily
Walking in the Aosta Valley
Walking in the Dolomites
Walking in Tuscany
Walking in Umbria
Walking Lake Como and Maggiore
Walking Lake Garda and Iseo
Walking on the Amalfi Coast
Walks and Treks in the Maritime Alps

IRELAND
The Wild Atlantic Way and Western Ireland
Walking the Kerry Way
Walking the Wicklow Way

EUROPEAN CYCLING
Cycling the Route des Grandes Alpes
Cycling the Ruta Via de la Plata
The Elbe Cycle Route
The River Loire Cycle Route
The River Rhone Cycle Route

INTERNATIONAL CHALLENGES, COLLECTIONS AND ACTIVITIES
Europe's High Points
Walking the Via Francigena Pilgrim Route —
Part 1
Part 2
Part 3

AUSTRIA
Innsbruck Mountain Adventures
Trekking Austria's Adlerweg
Trekking in Austria's Hohe Tauern
Trekking in Austria's Zillertal Alps
Trekking in the Stubai Alps
Walking in Austria
Walking in the Salzkammergut: the Austrian Lake District

MEDITERRANEAN
The High Mountains of Crete
Trekking in Greece
Walking and Trekking in Zagori
Walking and Trekking on Corfu
Walking on the Greek Islands — the Cyclades
Walking in Cyprus
Walking on Malta

HIMALAYA
8000 metres
Everest: A Trekker's Guide
Trekking in the Karakoram

NORTH AMERICA
Hiking and Cycling the California Missions Trail
The John Muir Trail
The Pacific Crest Trail

SOUTH AMERICA
Aconcagua and the Southern Andes
Hiking and Biking Peru's Inca Trails
Trekking in Torres del Paine

AFRICA
Kilimanjaro
Walking in the Drakensberg
Walks and Scrambles in the Moroccan Anti-Atlas

NEW ZEALAND AND AUSTRALIA
Hiking the Overland Track

CHINA, JAPAN, AND ASIA
Annapurna
Hiking and Trekking in the Japan Alps and Mount Fuji
Hiking in Hong Kong
Japan's Kumano Kodo Pilgrimage
Trekking in Bhutan
Trekking in Ladakh
Trekking in Tajikistan
Trekking in the Himalaya

TECHNIQUES
Fastpacking
The Mountain Hut Book

MINI GUIDES
Alpine Flowers
Navigation
Pocket First Aid and Wilderness Medicine
Snow

MOUNTAIN LITERATURE
A Walk in the Clouds
Abode of the Gods
Fifty Years of Adventure
The Pennine Way — the Path, the People, the Journey
Unjustifiable Risk?

For full information on all our guides, books and eBooks, visit our website:
www.cicerone.co.uk

CICERONE

Trust Cicerone to guide your next adventure, wherever it may be around the world...

Discover guides for hiking, mountain walking, backpacking, trekking, trail running, cycling and mountain biking, ski touring, climbing and scrambling in Britain, Europe and worldwide.

Connect with Cicerone online and find inspiration.

- buy books and ebooks
- articles, advice and trip reports
- GPX files and updates
- regular newsletter

cicerone.co.uk